RIPPLES

Ripples

3 Women,
1 Story
from regrets to blessings

PETRA COLE

XULON PRESS

Xulon Press
2301 Lucien Way #415
Maitland, FL 32751
407.339.4217
www.xulonpress.com

Paperback ISBN-13: 978-1-6628-6900-6
Ebook ISBN-13: 978-1-6628-6901-3

TABLE OF CONTENTS

Acknowledgments

To my oldest daughter, Monica, who I had the privilege of meeting years after her birth. Thank you for accepting me and letting me be a part of your world and family. It has been a joy becoming involved in your life, finding our similarities and differences, getting to know your family and being accepted by them, sharing stories of the years I missed and of course, our sweet conversations over the phone. I love you.

To my husband who once again never complained about my being holed up in my office, which he so graciously built for me. I so appreciate your encouragement and your patience, you are amazing to be married to! I don't anticipate another book in the future, but should there be one, it is you who I want to be living in the same house with as I write! You have been over the top understanding. Thank you. I hit the jackpot when I accepted your proposal!! I'd marry you again and again just to enjoy the life we have together, even with the ups and downs.

To my sister, Anne, for helping me to write yet a second book and for your part in participating by writing your side of the story of my pregnancy.

How God allowed me to have a sister like you is pretty incredible, I am beyond blessed. I look back at our growing up years and am thrilled you still claim me! Thank you, I couldn't love you more.

And thank you to my good friends, Trudy, Rene, Teri and Sue who allowed me to use the stories and pictures to share in my book. What would I do without you? You provided me with humor, solidarity, common sense and great company. Now if you would all move back so we can continue our saga!!! Sue, thank you for your hours of editing. No one knows how I love to use commas more than you!

Sally, thank you for being a huge delight in my life, for the challenges we have had and weathered, and the many times your humor has thrown me off balance in a delightful way. You have always kept me on my toes. I love you.

Foreword

I saw a picture posted online the other day with the caption 'unfiltered'. It was a beautiful sunset with a brilliant array of orange, gold and red colors highlighting the Cascade Mountains of the Pacific Northwest. On its own merit, the photo was striking. However, the photographer felt compelled to assure her audience that she didn't cheat. "No filter", as she declared promising that it was the real deal.

That's Petra Cole. She's the real deal. From the first time I met her, I was impressed by her no-nonsense approach to life. She says what she means, and she means what she says. No filters. Not brash, but honest. Not flippant, but whimsical. Petra has an authenticity about her that is compelling, refreshing and charming.

In my 28 years of Pastoral ministry, I have encountered scores of people who wear a mask to hide their true self. A painted-on smile to cover their sadness. A forced laugh to conceal their suffering. A new outfit to cover up their low self-esteem. Each one, a filter used to cover up the truth. To obscure the reality lurking below the surface. In my experience, people wear masks because of a question that haunts many of us: *if people knew the truth about me, would they still love me?*

<u>Ripples</u> is a refreshing look at an unfiltered life, told by a woman who is unafraid to show her true self to the world; scars

and all, because Petra knows that scars aren't something to be ashamed of. Scars tell stories. They tell about risks taken, relationships wounded, hearts broken and regrets remembered. And they also tell stories of redemption, forgiveness, reconciliation and healing. Those are the very ingredients that make life dynamic and worth living.

Petra tells her story of a life lived to the fullest. She pulls no punches. She tells it like it really is. She wears no mask and uses no filter to give us an unobscured view of herself and those whom she loves. It's a beautiful picture. Just like that unfiltered sunset, basking over the mountain range. It's a glimpse of God's masterpiece, meant to be enjoyed by all who would pause and take it in the way it was intended to be.

Jeff Poush
Associate Pastor
Salem First Baptist Church
Salem, Oregon

Introduction

I wonder how many times we look back on our life and think to ourselves, "What made me say that" or "Why did I even consider doing that?" My life has been full of those thoughts and I have to say that finally, getting older, I am saying it less and less. What a welcome relief. But it is those same questions that are causing me to write a second book. This book is about poor choices, acceptance, and unexpected joys. Looking back seems to offer us a real viewpoint of our errors and how we handled them. Sadly, while in the middle of creating a problem, we refuse to look at it for what it is. Instead, we make excuses until no more excuses are allowed, but decisions are made for us.

There is a part of my life that very few people know about. My first book was about my son and daughter whom I had the privilege to adopt. This book deals with an earlier part of my life where I gave a child up for adoption, by far the most difficult and heart wrenching experience I have ever gone through. The story needs telling because I am sure there are young girls/women having to make the same decision today. I hope as you read this you will get to know my heart, my determination to do the right thing, not the popular thing, and my desire to please my Heavenly Father who has greatly surprised me in His goodness in blessing me over and over again.

I want to begin writing about my early years as I remember much of them clearly and I want my readers to know how I was raised. My poor judgments were of my own doing, no-one else carries the blame except me. I was blessed with the family I was given.

As you read the events I have survived, the ones I took part in, and those that happened randomly that make life so much fun or very difficult, I hope you enjoy this book. I have certainly enjoyed writing it.

Prologue

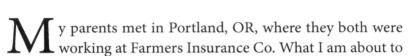

My parents met in Portland, OR, where they both were working at Farmers Insurance Co. What I am about to relay is the way I often heard their story from my father.

One day while I was in my office on the 2nd floor, this most beautiful woman came in needing to get some papers for her boss on the 1st floor of the same building. I could see her from the window in my office, so I started at her ankles and worked my way up, appreciating everything I saw. I came out of my office to be introduced to Harriet M. Hagen. That evening I waited for her outside the building to offer her a ride home. She said no. Being a determined man, this was not much of a discouragement. The second night I waited for her again, this time I convinced her to accept the ride, and she did. From then on , as the saying goes, it's just history. Meeting her parents was a huge success, they thought me a keeper in a very short time. Dinners, dates and adventures followed and finally, after asking Harriet to marry me several times, it was finally down the aisle for us!

According to my mom;
Dad was dating one of my best friends. My friends' younger sister wanted her sister to marry Ray, the man I had just met on the second floor where I worked at Farmers Ins. Co. I found him

to be very good looking, but taken. That evening, he was waiting for me to offer me a ride home. I said no. Actually, I was already engaged. The next evening, after a very convincing argument to accept his ride, I took it. Much to my surprise, my friend was not at all upset when I began riding home in Ray's vehicle, but my friends younger sister was furious that I was 'dating' him. I was not dating him, I was was just riding to my home in his car instead of on a bus. The sister of my friend never spoke to me again. Oh well. As I said, I was engaged to a man, George, who was in the service, so when Ray proposed, I told him until George, the man I was promised to, came home, I would not consider his proposal. I would not break off my engagement through a letter. By the time George returned, I had turned down Rays request for marriage one too many times and he had not asked me again. I broke off my relationship with George shortly after coming to Eagle Point to meet Rays large family. Shortly after, I asked Ray if his offer of marriage was still an option. He stopped the car, jumped out and started yelling "Whahoos" loudly. Then he got back into the car, opened the jockey box and took out the ring he had previously bought to give to me. It wasn't long before we were married! One of the best choices I have ever made.

After my parent's marriage, I was the second child to come along, the first being my brother, Rick, and then the third being my sister, Anne. I don't think I have the middle child syndrome, but it is definitely possible. I'd have to read again just what those characteristics are, but I don't seem to have any kind of syndrome, I certainly haven't found it yet!

CHAPTER 1

My Surroundings

The wind was rushing through our blonde hair, sometimes causing it to be hard to see exactly where the pounding hooves of our horse were taking us, but it was the need to reach safety that kept us spurring her on. Not sure of what came around the next corner, and hoping it would not be another form of dread, we kept riding. Passing the vast open ranges and slipping into the coolness of the rocky slopes allowed us a moment of hope. The greatest fear we faced was the large grizzly that had been spotted just a day or two before near where the herds of deer were passing through. We often came across Indians out on a hunt, but they were kind, not to be feared. The new chief had made peace with the surrounding villages and life had calmed down.

The air was dry, the sun shown down like a heat lamp on high setting, but the sky was as blue as a lapis stone. The day held much excitement that begged to be entered, and the two riders were very aware of their surroundings.

"Trudy, Petra, time to come in for lunch. Be sure to wash up and take your shoes off before you come in the house".

We hated having our adventure interrupted, but lunch was a real necessity. We were growing girls. Climbing off the large oil tank in Trudy's back yard, we headed in to lunch. The oil tank was the best horse we two young girls had! We talked about where we would ride next as we ambled toward the house. Life was so good and nothing was better than having a best friend who understood and lived for adventure. Every day counted to both of us. Not a moment to waste with so much going on in our small world of riding oil tanks, playing trucks and cars, building mud huts, and exploring everything there was in our back yard. The adventures were impressive.

Wait! I don't think three year olds actually think this way! If I were to be truly honest, it would be a few more years when we were actually riding real horses that we really began entering the life of mock endangerment and allowing our minds to run amuck.

(It would be more likely that they were simply cruising through the fields at a moderate pace...but were kicking the sides of the oil tank like they truly were headed someplace, right up until lunch was called. The horse would wait patiently for their next arrival time when they would remount and begin another stimulating adventure.)

When one meets their best life-long friend at such an early age, life-long takes on a whole new meaning. Seventy plus years later we would continue getting together taking trips, exploring new sites, and letting our memories wander. I find it ever so interesting that, as we age, we remember certain stories differently. Age can do that, but if the stories improve, I can't see the harm.

I grew up in the small southern Oregon town of Eagle Point. It's one of those places where you knew someone was a stranger simply because you didn't recognize them. A town where the retired men sat in front of the Post Office discussing the passing world and all of its problems, or possibly, the passing people and all of their problems. It didn't matter which it was, what mattered is that they belonged in front of the Post Office talking about things that mattered to them. My friends and I would ride into town on our bikes and comment, "There's so and so, sitting with so and so. Didn't we see them there yesterday and the day before?" It was a silly question because of course we all knew the answer before it was asked. We knew we would see those same men there tomorrow and the next day and every day we rode our bikes through town. It felt good to have things in place, that comfortable feeling that comes with repetition. Today, different men sit in the local restaurant because the Post Office changed location, but it's still the same gathering to exchange the most current gossip or discuss the current local news.

Once in awhile, if we had a nickel or dime, we would stop at Tina and Jake's combo burger place and drug store. Everyone knew them, and boy could they make good hamburgers. They also had ice cream cones for a nickel. That was before there was an actual ice cream hang-out in town. When Bud put in his ice cream/hamburger joint, I would ride my horse through town and stop in at the window for an ice cream. Bud would give me one for my horse as well, and we–meaning my horse and I–would take a break to enjoy our cones before heading home. I always found it amazing how my horse could finish a whole cone, ice cream and all, in 1 1/2 bites. The 1/2 bite took place because I was still holding the bottom of the cone and I was not about to be a part of the actual bite!

Often, I would stop at my grandmother's dress shop *The Town and Country Shop,* which was on the main corner of town. I would handle all the jewelry, admire anything new, and then get on my bike to head off elsewhere. My grandmother never

ever scolded me for touching things, but allowed me to handle and enjoy the beautiful jewelry. Some would be shimmering, and textured while others would be clear and smooth. At times, my grandmother would actually place a piece around my neck and allow me to wear it while I was in the store. I felt like a grown up, being allowed to wear such elegance. Prior to my mother's birthday, I would go to my grandmothers store (all of her many grandchildren called her 'Nannan) and hand her all the money I had saved–sometimes just coins, maybe a dollar or two, and I would ask her what I could buy for my mom. It just so happened that every time I shopped for my mom, there happened to be a special, a sale above all sales, going on. I might walk out with a dress, a lovely piece of jewelry, or a new hat that cost the exact amount I had with me. It would be beautifully wrapped and there would be a card for me to sign. I have no idea how old I was before I realized the true gift my 'Nannan' was giving me.

Later in life, when I got into playing tennis, my Nannan bought me a very stylish tennis outfit. I wore it proudly. I was quite tall and very slender, (some said skinny, but that's strictly hearsay). When she went to the Seattle market, Nannan often returned with a gift for me. She was several grades above the ordinary grandmother. She became the "Mother of the Year" for the state of Oregon. If "Grandmother of the Year" had existed, she would have easily won that as well.

My town itself was quite ordinary but the people living there made it wonderful. The town consisted of a few streets and a creek running through the middle with a single bridge to cross it. It was the homes filled with families that held the intrigue of the small town. Older people were often like grand-parents, even if there were no real family ties. They would speak to kids walking by, sometimes bringing out cookies and offering kool-aid when it was hot. Or they might ask for help in carrying in groceries or other heavy objects that presented them hardships and the kids were happy to oblige. Life was friendly in the small town and it was a wonderful place to grow up.

Mr. Putman's grain mill was on my way to school, and many days I would stop in to get a handful of this specific type of grain, that, when chewed, had the texture of gum. Mr. Putman was one of my favorite people, and on a hot day, he would take me in to the cool walk-in freezer just to cool down. The mill ran on a paddle wheel turned by the creek. It was a truly amazing place and it still exists today. It burned down in the early 2000's, but it was rebuilt and somewhat back in business some time later.

Tall trees lined Royal Ave. and I believe those trees absolutely were put there for kids to climb. You could climb high enough to see a very long way, and there was nothing better on a hot day than to sit in a cool tree. The roots of those trees tore up the sidewalk so it probably wasn't particularly safe for people walking. But for those of us on bikes, it was delicious! Bumps and jumps and large cracks… a bicycler's haven!!

Plus, while sitting in a tree, one could observe just what the neighbors were doing. Some might be mowing their lawns, others sitting on a chair just watching the clouds if there were any. On a really exciting day, we might catch someone arguing and listen in hoping for some juicy morsels of information. All to say, trees along the road made for some great times.

CHAPTER 2

Family Life

My mother was a piano teacher, my dad had a log truck business and worked on our grandparents ranch which our property butted up to. I loved music then and still do today. When I was 3, my mother would give a music lesson in our home, and after the student would leave, I would get up on the piano bench and play what I had just heard. Hence, I began lessons. God gave me a wonderful ability to never need music to play a piece, but my mother, for a long time, did not realize this. I would ask her to play what the song was going to sound like that she had given me for a lesson that week, and then when my mother left the room, I would sit and play the piece myself. By the time my mother realized I could not read music, but was only using my ear, piano lessons became extremely boring for me as I had been playing beyond what I was able to read and had to start over, learning to read actual musical notes. I learned that when I played a piece, I would add in notes that didn't exist, giving my mom the clue about my lack of note recognition. Later, when I became a music teacher I was big on music reading and theory so that would not happen to my students. I also had them write music very early to tap into their creativeness. It was a God given gift, one I shall enjoy up to my time to leave this world. Who knows, maybe there will be piano's in Heaven!

Rick age 5 1/2, Petra age 3. Taken in 1953

My parents, Petra and Rick 1953

I went to a private kindergarten at Mrs. Cunningham's home. It was a beautiful house out in the country. You entered by driving down a long driveway with a white fence on either side. Looked like a place out of a story book.

Most of the kids I went to kindergarten with also graduated high school with me. Kind of like family, we knew each other so long and so well. There is something special about growing up with the kids from kindergarten and keeping them as friends through high school graduation. To this day I am in contact with several of them.

One of my favorite occasions at kindergarten was coloring Easter eggs after which Mrs. Cunningham would hide them in the field. Have you ever hunted Easter eggs in a field? Not an easy task, unless you happen to step on them, but that certainly would not stop you from eating them. The grass was high, taller than any of us, and the hunt was a morning full of fun challenges, running around with no pattern in mind, chasing each other yelling and screaming and being totally carefree. There probably is no better schooling than learning how to negotiate friendships, giving and the taking, and learning that everything is not all about me. Those skills are greatly lacking in our education today. It has become more 'all about me' or it's considered wrong, hence the problems we are witnessing all around us. When the focus becomes 'me' centered, we have lost the focus of life.

My family all went to church on Sunday, youth group on Sunday evening, and often Wednesday night prayer time. Admittedly, I enjoyed Sunday School, but church was a very long sit. In fact, such a long sit that on occasion I would get into trouble for making excessive noise, usually in the form of laughter. One such Sunday, Trudy and I were sitting in the front row. I cannot recall what was said between us that struck us so funny, but holding in a laugh can actually be quite painful, I think maybe even harmful to your health, but we tried. Our shoulders were bouncing up and down, the tears were being shed from our eyes, and there was no way we could look at one another. Worse yet, Trudy's mom was in the choir sitting in front looking down at us and giving "the look " all kids understand. So, I just didn't look at her. Perhaps it was the little gasps that were sneaking out of us that caused my mom to come up from a few pews back, take me by my arm and lead me back sit beside her. Horrifying, humiliating, embarrassing, and noted by all in the church! Unfortunately, the laughing didn't quit. I absolutely could not help it. Little sounds kept escaping, which my mom did not find funny in the least. Every time I looked up I saw the back of Trudys head, and I'd lose it.

Now, you must understand, I didn't do this on purpose. But I couldn't convince anyone to listen to my reasons, probably because they were pretty lame. But that Sunday when we got home, I was punished. I wish I could say I learned my lesson, but a good laugh is something you just shouldn't walk away from, consequently there were a few more incidences over the years, but none too close together, (meaning weekly), that I recall.

Both my parents knew how hard it was for me to sit still. In fact, on a given day, my mom would reward me if I could sit on a chair for 5 minutes. She didn't have to reward me often because I didn't succeed often. It wasn't a form of punishment, in fact, it was a form of competition which I have always loved. But, not having someone else to sit on a chair beside me moved it out of the realm of competitiveness for me. Me versus me? I don't think so! That is why I was seldom rewarded, I needed someone to beat!

CHAPTER 3

Broadening My Horizons

Every year we had Bible Camp at Lake of the Woods. I loved Bible Camp, even though there were some very dramatic things that happened there. One perfect afternoon during our free time, I was engrossed in catching a curious chipmunk. I had food in my hand, and it was getting very close to leaping in to grab it. Within a wink of an eye, a large hawk swooped down and took the little guy from right before me. The anger rose up and I threw pinecones at it, threw dirt at it, I yelled, I threatened, but it was a total loss. I had to carry the knowledge that I had led that little chipmunk to his death. I would forever bear the responsibility for him. I still think about him, such a tragedy.

Other parts of camp were a little less notable, like keeping our cabin clean, freezing at the bon fire, dressing in the morning and having to dress while staying in the sleeping bag to avoid the cold. But we did have one evening that was special, when we dressed up more than the nights. My counselor's dress was hanging in the tent and, as my sense of humor had not yet fully developed, I thought it would be funny to hide her dress in a tree, in the wind. Something was very wrong with her hanger because her dress fell off onto the ground, and onto the dirt, leaves, branches, and pinecones. It was so filthy! I don't recall her being angry, but I also don't recall her having an over-whelming sense of humor either. Of course, I didn't mention that the night before we (Trudy and I) had filled her sleeping bag with pinecones and sewed her bag shut. In Trudys defense, I have to say I tended to be the one to come up with the ideas because Trudy was far nicer and more considerate than myself. BUT, she did go along with this suggestion, so being my cohort, she deserves some credit.

At camp in 1957, we had a young and very handsome speaker who was able to hold my attention. He had a strong faith and he talked about God, making life with God sound like the most exciting thing ever to the point that I believed him and accepted Christ to be my Savior. I wanted the life He had to offer me. I never have regretted that decision and as I continued to live life, I found I could not have lived it without the LORD. Best decision I ever made, and that would be proven over and over again. I know Trudy would say the same thing as she also accepted Christ that evening.

In our small town there was a girl who was an only child. Her name was Shelly. Actually, that's not her real name, but that's the name I am giving her. She was cute, smart, skinny and crazy about my brother. Now, being an only child with no brothers, she was a girly girl. I, on the other hand, did not think there was a boy stronger than myself and would go to just about any length to prove it. (One day many years later, I became the Jackson County Women's Arm Wrestling Champion!)

Shelly's mom made her a pink tutu and decided she would be thoughtful to make one for me as well. I, not being a tutu kind of girl, was horrified. I wore jeans, cowgirl skirts, boots, but not tutu's! My mother, on the other hand, wanting me to show my gratitude for the work Shelly's mom had done, required me to wear it while Shelly was at my home. I wanted to throw up but knew that would not be acceptable and the consequence of such a reaction would bring only pain, so I put on the tutu. Two very long skinny legs hung out from underneath a very frilly pink costume and I looked like a toothpick with a fluff ball around the middle. "Oh please help me! Eliminate this moment from my life, and whatever the future may bring, may no-one ever see me in this ridiculous outfit!" Thoughts ran rampant through my mind as I stood there imagining that life had just about ended at that very moment, and horrendous thoughts were forming as to how to make this incident never occur again. Maybe I could drown Shelly in our irrigation ditch, or get her on the back of my horse and run her under a low branch? Something had to be done, especially before my brother saw me in a pink tutu!

Like with most tragedies like this in life, there comes a time to get even. Mine came, and with my brothers help, the event went exactly as planned.

My father and grandfather had recently irrigated the pasture when Shelly called and asked what I was doing which was immediately followed by, "Is Rick home?" When I said that he was, Shelly was at our house within minutes.

I'm just curious at this point as to how many of you have had experiences with electric fences and water? My brother and I certainly were and had played many games of 'crack the whip' with other kids who chose to come and hang out with us. But with Shelly, both my brother and I were ready to take it to the next level.

Shelly arrived at the house in her very cute summer attire ready to play dolls or some such boring thing. My brother and I had a different game in mind. We explained to Shelly what an incredible feeling went through the body when one stood in water while holding on to the electric fence. I'm quite convinced that she would not have believed it if only I had made this statement, but my brother, whom Shelly thought was beyond the average catch, collaborated my story. We took Shelly (who happened to be barefoot) over to a place that was out of sight of our mother, and invited her to grab hold of the electric fence. Oh, if you could have heard the cry coming out of her mouth, you would understand why our mother came running out of the house with a look of absolute horror on her face. Shelly was shrieking and shaking as she continued to cling to the fence, not because she wanted to, but because she couldn't let go. Seeing what was happening, mom ran to the shed and shut off the electricity to the electric fence. This was a very exciting moment for me as a 9 year old and it set the scene for many more adventures to come. What strikes me as odd is, I can't even remember the punishment Rick and I received for our little incident. It must have been worth whatever it was, and I am sure this was one of the very few times my mother shared our shenanigans with our father. I'm sure it wasn't pretty, but we lived!

Forty of so years later, I was home visiting my mom. She told me a surprise visitor was coming so I was anxiously awaiting. When the doorbell rang, I answered but had absolutely no idea who was standing there. Finally having to ask her name, I said "Shelly"? Horrified, I wondered how in the world could I have any conversation with her with all the memories going off in my head. Should I apologize or should I first find out what she remembered? Fortunately, Shelly brought up the days we spent together and she only remembered such sweet stories. Why couldn't I remember any of those "sweet stories"? Guilt. It could only be because I was feeling guilty. Shelly didn't even remember the time I put her on our horse to give her a ride around the field. Putting my horse into a full gallup, I very suddenly pulled on the reins to make her turn quickly, forcing Shelly to either grab hold or fly off. She flew off, there was no time to grab hold. SHE DIDN'T EVEN REMEMBER THAT! (I want to add a disclaimer. I really was not a mean person, in fact, I don't know that I have a mean bone in my body. But something about what I perceived as being weak, mainly girls who were not tomboys, needed toughening up, and that was my job, to toughen her up!)

Instead, she was a beautiful woman with delightful memories. I was completely ashamed, but laughed at the shared stories. What does that say about me? If someone would have done those things to me, they probably would be missing some body parts! In fact, I find humor in remembering past times and have gone as far as to share many stories with others, laughing uncontrollably as I mentally relive them.

There are many stories that are based around my horse, Jingles. My family admired Jingles because of her intuiton and her love for me, Rick and our dad. One time, 4 year old Rick called her from the field. It had been raining and, as Jingles approached Rick, she could't stop so she reared up and come down straddling Rick, untouched. When I was small, I would stand on the fence to get on her. Occasionally, just as I was about to jump on her back, Jingles would take one step away, and I would miss. It seemed like a game to Jingles. One time she would stand still; the next time, move away. I also loved to gallup her in the field and jump downed trees or other objects but if I put my little sister on with me, Jingles would refuse to do more than a walk. As hard as I would kick her or cluck my tongue, nothing changed the pace. It's a great thing to grow up with a good horse.

We always knew when my dad was coming home. Jingles could tell the sound of his truck coming down the road and she would begin galloping up and down the pasture in anticipation of his arrival. The two of them had a wonderfully close relationship. When dad would pull in the driveway, Jingles would be standing where the truck would park, waiting for dad to get out and love on her. It was fun to watch.

I will never forget one time when Anne was throwing hay in little bunches to Jingles. She stood on the first rail of the fence and put her head through the second one to feed her. Anne's hair and the hay had a remarkable resemblance and Jingles took a hold of Anne's hair. Anne screamed, they both threw their heads back, Anne hitting the rail of the fence rather hard. I know it should not have been funny, but how could one not laugh? Poor Anne, poor Jingles!

Because we lived in the country outside a small town, both my parents felt it important that we learn about vehicles and driving at an early age. I was allowed to drive the tractor when I weighed enough to be able to put down the clutch and change gears. With the car, I was allowed to shift the gears as mom or dad put in the clutch. Often I would sit on the lap of my parent and drive. As I progressed, eventually on cold mornings, I was allowed to go out and start the car to warm it up. All I had to really remember was to make sure the gear shift on the column wiggled to confirm that I had it in neutral.

My grandpa had a gas tank at his home, so instead of going to a filling station, mom would drive up the road to my grandpa's place to fill the car. On one such morning, after she had backed up to the pump, I was sitting in the car waiting for mom as she filled the tank. As she was finishing, I reached over to start the car, not checking the movement of the shift. It had been left in reverse gear, so when the motor started, the car began moving backwards. Mom was caught between the irrigation ditch and the gas pump. Life does have a way of flashing before you, and I knew in my mind I had just ran over my mother. In a panic, I crawled under the front car seat. I believe I was about 5 at this time. My grandfather had been watching out the window and came running out. By the time he came to check on me, he had already rescued my mom and taken her in his house. I had assumed the worst and was in a state of shock when he came back for me. It took me some time to hear him explain that the pump had fallen over so mom had been trapped between the pump and the car tire. She was fine. She had not been run over by the car nor had she drowned in the irrigation ditch. She was waiting for me inside. This is the first of many miracles that occurred in my life. I know the gas pump was in concrete, so there is no way it should have fallen over, but it did ! God is good. Miracles do happen. So often we allow them to slip by without recognizing them or thanking God for them. To this day I thank Him for this one. The story doesn't stop there though. My parents modeled wise parenting so instead of banning me from starting the car on cold mornings, I was taught more about how a car runs, and began to help take care of the car more. I was never punished, only made more aware of the dangers along with the positives regarding cars. By the age of 12 I was allowed to drive alone to get milk from the dairy and to run a few other errands for my parents. Responsibility is a great confidence builder.

My brother was two and a half years older than me, and we had a love/hate relationship growing up. Not really hate, but at times close to it. One of the games I loved playing with him was, for lack of knowing what to call it, "acting out an animal who was always a protective beast". We would go through the World

Book of Knowledge 'wild cat' section and pick out a very dangerous wild cat for Rick to become. Maybe a black panther, lion, tiger, or even a cougar. Then we would create situations where he, being the wild ferocious cat, would have to protect me. Oh the battles that took place between Rick and the unseen enemies were horrific, keeping me on the edge of my seat just hoping the outcome would be in Rick's favor. He never ceased to be astonishing in his ability to fight and win. Such a hero in an animal there will never be again. If it were not for his courageous actions, I may have not been writing this story. Thank you big brother.

We had some wonderful neighbors that didn't live far from us. Boys, the best kind of neighbors. They had a fort, a real fort that made the perfect place for the calvary to live. Out in our field was a stand of trees which made a perfect place for the Indians to live. The battles between the Indians and the Calvary were intense. Surprise attacks, wars, and occasionally, an offering of peace. It can all happen, and did in an afternoon. I remember one time I was strapped on the horse, stomach across our horses back, and my horse was hit on the rump so it would gallup back to the calvary's location. Something about that ride was not as comfortable as I had first thought it was going to be. My head seemed to bang around a lot...but it was fun. More than that, it kept the boys allowing me to play with them. They were into real fun, not hung up on dolls or tea parties. They built roads for their trucks, bridges across the irrigation ditch, used slingshots, played at the creek, all the fun stuff and I wasn't about to miss out!

Johnny and George, our two neighbor boys, were over to play trucks often. I got to play because I made the best roads. I could angle a curve perfectly with the side of my hand. We played with sturdy trucks, ones that could withstand rough roads, fallen trees, and sudden surprises. Our imaginations made everything come to life; the word 'boring' was absent when we were playing. (To be perfectly honest, we learned early to never use the word "boring". My father or mother were both very capable of pulling up a to-do list to remove our "boredom", and there was no playing until the list was completed.)

Around the age of 5, another occurrence took place that altered my life. I learned my first really bad word. The situation was one of total innocence, and you will understand as this unfolds. Our neighbor who had no children, had a nephew who was from the city of Portland. Portland was way ahead of us when it came to using crude language. This neighbor and about 10 other people came to my parents house for a pinochle party and since Ricky, the neighbors nephew, was visiting, he come over to play with Rick and I. All the parents were in the house enjoying their evening playing pinochle while Rick, Ricky and I were outside enjoying our new toy, a refrigerator box. (Do you realize how many different things a refrigerator box can be? Well you ought to take some time just to jot down some things and go and enjoy being creative.)

We were playing in the box when Ricky asked Rick a question in a rather secretive manner. I was brought into the discussion shortly after. Ricky had introduced the "F" word to Rick and they decided to get me into trouble. Ricky told me that if went in to the house and said the "F" word to my father, I would probably get an ice cream or something good. That sounded like a win to me and so I marched into the house, right up to my dad, and blurted out that word which I won't even spell out! I had a very wise father who immediately understood that a 5-year old living in our area was highly unlikely to just come up with that on her own. He asked me where I heard it and I responded

"Rick and Ricky taught me." The place had become rather quiet and I was aware that something was not right. My father simply explained I was to never again use that word because next time I would be punished. Then asked me where he could find Ricky and Rick and I told him they were in the refrigerator box. My father calmly left the room, but what I heard next could have put the fear of God into me, but I already had it! Both boys were experiencing what they had hoped would happen to me! Imagine that. I was too young to understand then, but not too many years later the whole thing became very clear.

We had, and still have, a very large extended family as my father is from a family of 8 kids. All of them lived close enough for us to get together often at my grandparents' house, and when we gathered there, the first place we would head was to the barn.

Grandpa and dad kept loose hay in the barn along with ropes hanging from the rafters and stuffed gunny sacks we'd use to slide down the hay. The cousins would be out there doing their best tricks and showing off for the younger ones. The only time we left was for meal time, quickly returning to play. I had such a crush on several of my cousins. Three brothers, Warren, Lynn and Norman, were all cute, fun, and several years older than I was. I could have married any of them and been happy. Course, when you are 4, 5, or 6, that all makes great sense.

Some tragedies occurred during grade school. A major one for me was losing my two front teeth and having them grow back bucked. I had already dealt with scarlet fever and survived, now it was bucked teeth. Actually not only bucked teeth but I was pigeon-toed too and needed to wear ugly corrective shoes at that. At night, I would have to put on a pair of shoes connected by a metal bar to turn my feet out. It was impossible to roll over making it difficult to sleep. The option given to my parents was to break my legs and reset the bones. Fortunately my parents didn't consider that option for which I am so grateful.

Because I had to wear corrective shoes I was limited in the number of pair I had. One, to be exact. One day my father asked my mom to take me to town and buy me the most beautiful patent leather shoes she could find. This was a celebration time; I was getting a real pair of shoes, ones that would not stick out and shout, "Look at me" except for their beauty. Although I was only allowed to wear them on Sunday to church, it was such a treat. I felt I was a normal child every Sunday. They were beautiful, they shined, and my feet were simply stunning when I wore them. I don't think anyone noticed the feet turning in; they were all dazzled by my beautiful shoes. It's amazing what a pair of shoes can do to one's outlook on life, and how they can change the judgement of others toward one. I was a princess on Sunday, and just an ordinary kid wearing clunky shoes the rest of the week. Oh well, one day a week was far better than no days a week.

Mornings were a struggle after my teeth came in because we had very strict rules in our home, one being to chew with our mouth closed. I could not. My mouth would not close as I chewed. My brother, who sat at the opposite end of the table from me, would stack cereal boxes up between us trying not to see me or hear me as I ate. I would cry, or get mad, or both! And then when he would call me 'Bucky Beaver', all hell would break loose. I had no problem taking him on because he had one major weakness when it came to a fight. He had an extremely tender head. All I had to do is grab one handful of hair and hang on, for a sure win. Problem came when it was time to let go…I needed a parent around then for my protection! In time, when my teeth had finished growing in, I was ushered into the uncomfortable world of braces. As much as I hated braces for the entire four years I wore them, I have beautiful teeth today because of them. It is so nice to live in a time where braces were available. I can't imagine having to sit behind cereal boxes today!

From the beginning of Trudy and my friendship, our mom's made us dresses to wear to school. (Pants on girls were not allowed in school). We looked alike, dressed alike, and were inseparable. This caused concern to the teachers because we did almost everything together, so they decided to separate us into different classes for our social health. We still spent a lot of our weekends at one or the others house. When I was at Trudy's home, we spent quite a bit of time on her horse, Shorty. I don't recall Shorty being short at all, in fact, he was quite a tall, white horse that was ever so gentle. We would get under a laurel tree, which we renamed 'monkey tree' and, standing on Shorty's back, reach for the highest branch we could. Giving Shorty a kick to move him out of our way, we would bounce up and down on the branch until it was time to let go or get hung up in the tree. It was so much fun and being a kid was the best.

Trudy lived by a 60 acre, 60 foot deep, man-made lake which her father built prior to their moving up to the 1200 acre property. It was perfect for skiing, swimming, fishing, tanning and salamander hunting. Many summers we would swim across the lake, pushing the dock to get it to the other side for the summer. We rarely thought about the sun exposure and would end up with sunburns almost every year. Eventually we would have a beautiful dark tan. At the end of the day we hung our swimsuits on the deer horn outside the door so we had to be very careful the next day to check all areas of our swimwear for little creatures that might be waiting in them. Right down to the frogs!

Trudy also lived in a genuine log cabin. It was chinked, taking round logs which were then prepared by her parents. Her dad would cut the tree, her mother would take the bark off, and in the evening, her father would raise the log making walls for their home. Eventually, Trudy got her own bedroom above the garage. She would have to go out the back door, down the stairs, across a short area, and up the stair that led above the garage. More than once she felt she had to outrun a bear, beat a cougar, or go daintily around a skunk. There was always a boogie man or animal that prevented a safe feeling crossing to the stairway that led to safety. I know all this because I experienced it with her….standing on the stairs leading from the main house to the stairs leading to her bedroom, we talked about the dangers we might encounter. Strange that her parents never worried about us or watched to be sure we were safe. They must have lacked the creativity it takes to imagine all the 'possibilities' lurking.

Then there was the spillway. In the winter when the spillway froze, it was perfect for sliding down on an inner tube or a board. We were not allowed to do so but that did not stop us. What a ride it was, heading down the ice. We slid around corner to corner, did our best to avoid logs or large rocks, and screamed as we went on for miles, (gross exaggeration) at least long enough to be a little scared and end up finally in the field. We did get into trouble but, once again, it was so worth it. The 3 or 4 feet pool of water at the mouth of the spill-way also frooze and the ice got thick enough to pull us into another adventure. Trudy had a push peddle tin car that we would ride down the hill until we hit the ice, then slide around and around, slamming on the brakes to put us into a real spin before being stopped on the other side.

Trudy and Petra, approximately 1954

Trudy (left) and Petra, first day of school, 1956.

I lived in a one room house. It was built to be a garage someday, but for my first seven years we lived in it. I loved the closeness; everyone was in the same room, although my parents had a curtain separating their bed at night. My brother and I slept on couches, and it worked perfectly. We often had our friends over for the night, as adding another body or two was quite agreeable with my parents. We did have a single closet that all of our clothes fit in and a bathroom that had a door. I think about that today and feel sad that there seems to be expectations to have far more than needed. I'm sure I fall into that as well as I live in a lovely home. The most difficult part of living in what we always termed "the little house" was, when one person got sick, we all experienced the event, and usually followed suit.

After Rick and I entered school, my mom had a talk with dad. She wanted one of 3 things; to go to work, to have a larger home, or to have another baby. To her surprise, dad chose another baby, providing that she would never ask to have another. And, better yet, there was no more room in our little home, so dad began building another just a few feet away. I don't think my mom ever considered the size of our bathroom in our little house when she choose to get pregnant. But she soon found out, about 8 months later, that it was going to be a challenge to maneuver in. I remember quite well mom having to call dad for some help one evening. In our small bathroom was also our washer and dryer, causing a rather small entry. Mom had tried to enter by turning sideways and was stuck. Her stomach was up against the washer, her back against the side of the shower. Dad laughed, which may not have been the best response, but he was able to get mom unstuck and safely to her destination.

Anne was born in October and we moved into our new home in April. I did not like it because we were all separated by rooms. I loved being all together but things were changing. My brother had his own bedroom, mom and dad had their own room, and Anne and I shared a room. Our bathroom was huge, felt like it could have been its own apartment! I think it was quite some time before I appreciated having a home which seemed so big. It was built around a very large fireplace. Our kitchen and family room was on one side, the living and dining area on the other. This made for the perfect game of tag since there were entries on either sides of the fireplace to the various rooms. One day, dad and I were playing tag, and to take a short cut, dad attempted to jump over the chair after coming around the corner but he missed. He went down taking the chair with him. There was a moment of silence as we waited to see if he was able to move but fortunately he was not injured. All I could do was laugh, and he joined me soon as he himself knew he was not injured. My dad was so much fun.

We did not usually allow the animals in the house, nobody wanted to clean up the possible mishaps. My friend had given me the perfect "throw-up" gag gift. It looked so real! I laid it beside dads chair and that evening when he was sitting down to read the paper, he noticed the "throw up" and asked who had let the dog in the house. He told me to get something to clean it up with. I did. As I was cleaning it up with an old rag, I tossed it into his lap. In his hurry to get away from it, he threw himself backward, again tipping over the chair. I could see the color begin to raise until he saw the yuck still all contained in the same form it had been on the floor. I loved it when he laughed, he had a very infectious laugh and that is exactly what he began doing! He certainly enjoyed a good joke as he was one to give a good joke whenever he could.

Every rule seems to have an exception, which I think is a good thing, causing us to think outside the box. My dad could see this, and many times reacted in a way I wasn't expecting. Rick and I learned that if we did something majorly wrong, we would approach dad, he seemed to understand the drastic errors better than mom. If we just did something stupid or silly, we would tell mom because that never seemed to bother her. Dad loathed stupidity; mom detested major 'bads'.

I must have been around 8 when I first began going to Fortuna, Calif. to spend part of my summer with my cousin, Karen. She was about as fun a person that has ever existed! We were both tomboys and loved being outdoors exploring whatever there was to explore. One of our favorite things to do was have mud ball fights with her 3 brothers, Rod, Brad and Jay. We were in one 'fort', the boys in another. Karen and I would gather mud from the creek and round it into nice mud balls and the wars would began. Karen and I figured out that if we put a rock in our mud ball, they would hurt more, possibly causing the boys to surrender more readily. Our minds never stopped working!

At night, while in bed, we sang in harmony, "The Great Ship Titanic". Our nights were destined for sleeping. They were made for extending the day longer. The only difference was we were required to remain in bed, not run and roam. As we would sing, it gradually became louder. I know this because my Aunt Jeanne would eventually yell up to us to be quiet. Karen and I would just move ourselves under the covers and continue to sing. I do recall being separated for a night until we could grasp the rules of bedtime and understand the word, 'quiet'.

I loved waking up in the morning since it was the beginning of a new adventure. When one has a cousin like Karen, time moves too quickly and 'downtime' is an unknown word because downtime never happens. We remained close, even as we got older and responsibilities at home kept us from spending summers together. But once we started driving, we had occasion to visit again. One summer while I was in Fortuna, Karen and I decided to go to the Ferndale Fair where the parking lot was a field. I have no idea whose pickup we were driving but we got it parked and had a great day enjoying everything the fair offered, until our money ran out or we had eaten enough dust. When we got back to the pickup, we found it hemmed in by two vehicles. Whether there were no other parking places or they thought they would be out before us we couldn't determine, but it was definitely an untimely thing to do. I don't think Karen cared because she already had the solution. There may, for the ordinary person, have been a problem getting out, but not with Karen, not with how her mind worked. My job was to be the lookout! And for what, was my question to her. Simply put, for anyone running towards us in the field! That made perfect sense!! Why would we have to worry about anyone running towards us in the first place? Getting into the pickup, Karen put it into low gear, edged up to the first vehicle in front of us until the bumpers touched. Then she began pushing it til it was completely out of her way. If I recall correctly, this action hemmed in another car on the other side of the open driving space. Meanwhile, I'm still thinking about what I was to do if I saw someone running towards us. I knew Karen already had the solution, and I was afraid to ask. I knew it would be something like "hang off the tailgate and cover the license plate with your foot so it can not be ID'd". Not sure, but I may have been praying at that time for a huge bank of fog to protect us!

So now we had one car out of the way, and we could have left, but Karen, being the fair person she was, began backing up until she felt the bumper of the vehicle behind us. We then began pushing it across the parking lot to, most likely, hem in yet another car. Then, we left! That was life with Karen. I think part of her actions could have been from having three brothers. But then again, she was the oldest, maybe they became a product of her!

Karen married a great man, Ralph, and they had almost 50 years together before she died in May of 2022, I was blessed to be with her and her family at the time of her death. I have no doubt there was a lot of cheering and dancing in Heaven with her arrival. She truly was, and always will be, one of a kind.

Dad was in his truck coming out of the mountains when he came across a doe that had been hit. He stopped to take her off the road and found she was actually in the process of birthing. The mother, being dead, made my father decide to bring the fawn home. We called him Bambi until we found we would have to change that to Bambette, since it was a girl, a baby doe. Our dog and that fawn played together every day; it was an experience of a lifetime. At this time I had a white Volkswagen that I dearly loved, and both the fawn and our large dog would get in the back seat and ride into town with me, heads hanging out the front window. It wasn't long before the deer could no longer fit in the Volkswagen, so I had to take the pickup where both could ride in the back. I loved seeing all the people point and comment on my load. I said earlier that my parents did not like to have the animals in the house, but there was one exception.

Both the fawn and our dog were allowed to come into the house when the TV show, Lassie, was on. They were mesmerized by it. They would sit in front of the television glued to the program. Sadly, I only have one picture of them doing that but what a wonderful memory.

In time we moved Bambette up to Trudy's family's place where she had much more room to roam. For several years, after giving birth to her fawns, she would bring them back to Trudy's house to show off her little ones. She usually gave birth to twins. Eventually, she quit showing up. Whether she was forgetting her human family or something else happened we never would know.

Besides Bambette, we also raised a young coyote for awhile. Our horse would have nothing to do with it because of the smell of being a wild animal. Our cows neither. But it was so much fun, played just like a puppy and had a sweet personality. Unfortunately we did not know that a baby coyote will actually eat himself to death, and that is exactly what happened, too much dog food.

My little sister was smart from day one. She definitely took after my mother in that area. Not saying my dad was not smart, but my mom was brilliant. My being 7 years older than Anne also made her a nuisance from my point of view. One of her favorite things to do was, in the morning, run into the living room where I would be sitting, jump into my lap, and blow her bad breath in my face and say, "Whhh-morning". I'm not sure why, but she loved to do this often and I found it rather gross. Unbrushed teeth breath, no thank you. Imagine that overnight smell of ones breath wafting through the air and entering your nostrils. It's enough to cause unkind thoughts to run unrestrained through the brain.

Anne was as honest as the day straight. I had to be careful what I said and what I did around her because she would give a full report to my parents. I took care of that in my later teen years, after I had my own car. My father bought me a Volkswagen which I dearly loved and drove everywhere a car should not go. I would load Anne into the car when she would have a secret on me, and take her to the top of the hill above the lake by our home. I would have her look down the hill at all the tall, solid trees, and finally at the very blue sparkling lake. I would slowly begin driving down the grassy hill right at trees and tell her to promise that she would not tell on me. As I headed for a tree, she would see that I was going to crash us into it if she did not promise, and she would yell, "I promise, I promise, I promise not to tell". I would, of course, avoid that tree but head for another, making her once again promise. It was a tense and splended experience. I would do this all the way to the bottom of the hill stopping with both front tires in the lake. Amazingly, this worked and I don't think she ever told on me. I'm so glad she didn't figure out that I wasn't willing to die and would never consider putting a dent in my car. That must have been from my 7 more years of life wisdom that she had not yet experienced.

Eagle Point and Halloween were perfect; a small town with lots of excitement! One of the favored tricks was the purse on a string. One year we were hiding in the ditch with the purse out in the street when a car, which had a Police Officer following behind, stopped so suddenly the officer almost hit her. We were laughing so hard and pulling the purse back to remove the evidence while listening to the woman explain to the officer why she had suddenly stopped. No purse, no evidence. Other times we would be in a tree overhanging the road and drop tomatoes on cars going by. I recall a time when, for some reason, police officers chased my brother and some of the other boys out into our field. One of the boys fell into the ditch and had to quietly stay there to not be caught, even though it was very cold. There was just something fun about that time of year and I would be willing to bet that even the police had fun. We never did anything to harm or destroy things, just fun pranks.

The other date that we all loved was the 4th of July. Our parades went on and on. Horses, floats, trucks, bands, organization representations, more horses… it was great. The streets would be crowded with people everywhere. As the parade would pass by our home, we had hoses stretched out to the road ready to soak those in the parade. When the fire truck would come by, they would open up their hoses and soak US!! How I loved our small town. Booths, games, rodeo's, that day was the best, ending with fireworks. We would leave in the morning, then get home in the afternoon to enjoy a BBQ and homemade ice cream. After the eating was over, it was time for Annie Annie Over and, later in the evening, Hide and Go Seek.

CHAPTER 4

Moving Ahead

After what I would call a nearly perfect childhood, I entered adolescence. I finally got out of my corrective shoes, and styled myself with braces on my very bucked teeth. Before they could put on the braces, I had to have five teeth pulled. I have to say that was not the most fun I have ever had. Today I have those five teeth in a jewelry box; they really don't look too bad outside the mouth! When the orthodontist put the braces on me, they really hurt but being able to see the difference in my appearance within a year made them acceptable. It was almost five years before I finally got them removed, revealing absolutely straight, beautiful white teeth. I couldn't smile enough after that!!

It was the summer of my 8th grade year, I had my first boyfriend. I had a lot of boy friends, but a real boyfriend was altogether different. All my girl friends had already had a boyfriend, if not several. So now I could be one of them. I met him at a party at Trudy's home. He was from a town not too far from Eagle Point and the school he attended merged with Eagle Point for high school. This young man was outdoorsy, charismatic and liked to ride motorcycles, as did I. It was the charismatic that got me into trouble because I wasn't used to the 'charismatic' attitude towards me. I bought into it hook, line and sinker. I was not used to being told I was pretty, even though my teeth were getting quite straight by now. My father would tell me I was pretty but he was my father so that certainly didn't count as he was supposed to tell me things like that.

This young man and I didn't see each other over the summer, but in the fall we met up again in high school. We began doing things together, going to dances, high school games, lunch or dinner at our parent's homes, hunting and hiking. We had a great time, both of us enjoying adventure. He taught me how to scuba dive in the Rogue River where we dove for fishing lures. We would find some pretty amazing ones and it sure beat having to buy them. We continued to date off and on for the next several years. I say off and on because he was not what one would call a 'faithful' date and he had many dates behind my back that I would find out about later. But I, on the other hand, was quite faithful. After all, in my mind there may not be another boy who would look at me twice.

Having a low opinion of myself was a definite problem I carried. My father was my best cheerleader when it came to building me up. Once when I was younger and my mom was trying to teach me how to cook, dad came into the kitchen to find me crying as I was listening to instructions. He convinced my mom to let me become engaged in what my natural bent was. Cooking was, and continues to be, pretty low on my list of likes. My dad began teaching me how to chop wood, which eventually grew into how to use a chainsaw, and I helped cut and split our winters wood supply. I was in heaven! I also cleaned out the barn, helped milk the cows, and learned how to garden. As long as I wasn't lazy, I did not have to be in the kitchen.

My father also took me on father-daughter dates where we went to a restaurant called Bambi's in Medford. We ordered chocolate sundaes with an extra cherry on top. I should have been satisfied with all my fathers encouragement, but he was, as I said, my father. He was supposed to love me and think that I was special because I belonged to him.

I know my dad knew what was going on in the head of the boy I was dating, and dad tried to protect me from him. But instead, I began to rebel. If dad said to be home by midnight, I would stand on the door stoop until 12:05, knowing I would be grounded. It gave me a reason to stand up to my dad, and why I even went down that path, I don't know.

One Sunday morning we were walking to church as a family and I refused to walk beside my father. I walked several steps behind, but never beside. My mother told me years later that the only time she had ever seen my father cry was that Sunday when we got home. He told her he knew he could not give in to the rules he had set up because I would just continue to rebel against any rule he made. He knew he had to remain consistent, but that it hurt more than he ever imagined. Today, as I write this, tears stream down my eyes. How insensitive, how uncaring, how selfish I acted. It would not be long before I came to understand just how much my father and mother loved me and it would be the most difficult lesson I would ever have to learn. I have the greatest respect for my fathers choice to remain consistent rather that to try to buy my love through giving in to my wants. He was a real father, a father that wanted the best for all of his children, a man who sacrificed his own emotions to try to save me from a disaster. What a gift I was given and ignored altogether until two years later.

Just some thrown in thoughts. Why is it so hard to accept someones suggestions when they have already lived their life past your own years? Why can we not see how much someone really loves us when the advice they give us is for our own good? What I lacked in wisdom, my parents were ready to provide but my excuse for not listening was always the same, "They are not me!" No, they were much smarter, much more caring than I was; they were trying to help me avoid mistakes where I was full scale running into them.

Oh to have wisdom when we are young, to trust the words of those that care, to be bold enough to allow the hurt of walking away instead of plunging into a hurt that is hard to ever recover from. I watch it over and over in young lives and understand far more than I wish I did.

Toward the end of 1966, my junior year of high school, I knew something was wrong. My period, which were normally regular, didn't arrive. I didn't think of the possibility of being pregnant, but instead went down the line of having cancer. That was the disease common to our familly on my mother's side. When I told mom, she set up an appointment with the doctor for me to have a check-up. The results were unexpected. They came back saying I was pregnant. Are you kidding me....pregnant? How could I be pregnant? The few times we were together in an intimate way, he had used a condom. I called the doctor a liar and left the doctors office in my own car. I was angry and unwilling to accept what I had just been told. And I was in shock. When my mother got home, she shared with my father that I was pregnant. I did not go home, instead I went to the place I used to take my sister in my Volkswagen to make her swear to keep secrets. I sat on the hilltop, looking over the lake below trying to decide what my choices in life now were. I knew abortion was not a choice, I knew suicide was not a choice, but what was there other than that? I sat there and thought of the guilt I had always carried after I would give in with my boyfriend. The foolishness of thinking he really cared when he had sex as part of his plan. I knew it was wrong, but I had always thought "it could never happen to me" when it came to pregnancy. I hated the guilt, but I was taken in by being desired. If only I had been smart enough to know it wasn't "me" he loved. It was what I had to give. 'I' could have been anyone.

It wasn't until dark that I headed home. Mom, I found out later, had been afraid when I didn't come home that I might have chosen to end my life. I understand that fear, but it was not one she needed to consider.

As I drove in our driveway, I was prepared for my father's wrath. I had deliberately and outwardly created such a gap between us that I expected him to react like I would have. I was already making plans in my mind for where I would live once my father kicked me out of the house. I was thinking of ways to pass the blame, to call it a rape, but that would have been a lie. I walked into the house and dad was sitting on the hearth waiting for me. In anger, I asked him if mom had told him I was pregnant? His response was to put his arms around me and just hold me. No anger, no raised voice, he just held me. Every ounce of rebellion left me in that moment, and I felt every ounce of love he was pouring into me. Then he softly said, "Sometimes it's good to hit rock bottom because the only way left to go is up." If there was a moment in my life that I understood the love of God, it was then. My father was imitating his Heavenly Father, and my Heavenly Fathers love for his children. God became real to me and I witnessed the healing power that comes with faith, a healing that was complete and overwhelmingly wonderful.

There is nothing as wonderful as being reconciled with someone so very important in your life. For me it was my father, and my Heavenly Father.

Petra, 16, Rick, 18, and Anne, 9–1966

CHAPTER 5

The Ripples Begin; Anne's story

W hen I decided to write this book, it was because my oldest daughter, Monica, had asked me to write her story. Thinking about how I would write it, I knew just my input would not be nearly as effective as to also have those who had been greatly effected by my pregnancy to include their story. So beginning with my little sister, Anne, this is how her world changed due to my sin. Being seven years younger than myself, she was at the place where life didn't have boyfriends or other harmful pulls on it. So as you read her account, imagine a 9 year old from a secure home, well loved, having to hear the predicament her family was about to experience.

Anne's story

It was an interesting evening when mom asked me to snuggle with her in bed. As we were talking, mom brought up what had happened to my older sister, Petra. She told me my sister was pregnant and how she got pregnant. The 'how' part was a bit shocking and not fun to hear from her. I cried, mostly because mom was sad. I truly had no understanding why the sadness, but I did understand that

I didn't like her telling me about all the body parts. I didn't like hearing how babies were made.

To me, Petra was always so beautiful and stylish, having the latest hairdo, new make up, eyeliner, and I enjoyed watching her put it all together in front of the bathroom mirror. We were a family of 5 with one large bathroom so there was little privacy. It seemed she got all the new clothes, too! Well, we spent quite a bit of time at the fabric store looking at patterns and fabric. Looking back I see that she and mom were finding patterns that would disguise her growing body. I just liked it because it was fun. I remember the fabric search once they found the perfect pattern. Vogue patterns were known as the most complicated but that is what they usually picked. Only a few were Butterick or Simplicity. The ones they picked were always so stylish and pretty!! Our mom sewed and I'm sure our Nannan did also. I loved her new gorgeous clothes and thought it was really a neat thing to have such a "model" for my sister.

Honestly, I don't remember much interaction with Petra the next months. I remember many of her beautiful magazine perfect dresses and hair styles. Mom, dad and Rick, in hindsight, kept me sheltered with life as normal as possible. My best friend, Pammy, still came and went, we worked on our log cabin and we stayed innocent 9 year olds.

One afternoon I was walking home from school, via Brunners Grocery Store and an older sister of one of Petra's friends started walking by me. She started saying what I considered mean things about Petra and my family. She teased and taunted me and I got mad at her. I know I

didn't say "shut-up" because I had my mouth washed out
with a bar of soap for saying that to our mom, but I know I
said something to her and ran away. I didn't talk to her for
many years until she asked me to babysit for her. I agreed
to do that because her husband was so kind. I didn't tell
anyone about her mean-ness because I didn't want to
make them sad, plus I could take it myself, I was sure!

Dad was a self employed logger and his truck was
backed into our driveway each evening. My favorite,
almost nightly, ritual was to sit on the safety chains that
dangled at the back of his truck and ride while he backed
his truck to the parking spot. I say this because I vaguely
remember discussions at the dinner table and my inability
to ride the chains for several nights. His truck had been
vandalized one night and I think some tires were slashed.
Having a pregnant teenaged daughter brought out the
ugly in a few people, but not in our family.

I knew that I was not to tell people about the baby
and that was fine. If I ever had questions or something to
say, I could talk to mom, dad or Rick easily. I don't think
I ever did. But, when my 9 year old self heard that mom
told her friend, Marvel, and our Nannan, I was furious! I
couldn't believe that she told anyone and for a bit I considered her "betrayal" as the worst offense possible. I
had no understanding of the prudence or need of telling
them. I just knew I never even told Pammy and took moms
inability to keep a secret very serious. In time I understood she had betrayed no one and it was important for
her closest friend to know the situation, especially for
encouragement, support and prayer. The same for our

Nannan, especially since we were moving away for the last months of Petra's pregnancy.

Mom told me that we would move for the summer to a new place with a pool. I was excited!! I never knew that they had been looking for a place near the doctor Petra was seeing, nor that she was seeing a doctor! I just knew we were on a fun adventure. Later I heard that dad insisted that the apartment, or house, must have a pool so we'd (me) have some active fun. I loved apartment living! Rick and dad come on the weekends which meant more fun for me. Rick gave me diving lessons which, for the most part, were wonderful. We worked a lot on the jackknife dive going up as far a possible and coming down as close to the board and straight, which also meant very little splash. One time I got too close to the board and hit my boney knees hard on the board. I think Rick was in the water about the same time as I hit the water. I remember him helping me out of the pool. I was crying and mad that he made me hit my knees! I think I had to do the jackknife 5 more times right afterward so I wouldn't be afraid. Then we started on the swan dive lessons.

Often at night, I would hear Petra crying. It made me so sad for her yet I really had no understanding of her sadness. I don't think we ever talked about it. I was very naïve and probably self absorbed.

Apartment living was full of adventures for me. One neighbor practiced the piano for hours daily and she was good. Every day she warmed up by playing "Flight of the Bumble Bee" and it became a favorite. Petra could play it without practice just by listening to it. I later learned to play it but it took hours of practice. At nine, I thoroughly enjoyed living amongst the different people, saying hello to most and looking through their windows. I missed Pammy and Nannan, but leaving Eagle Point wasn't a big deal. At the apartment, we ate smaller meals since it was just the three of us. There were more salads than normal for dinner. I didn't think much of that until the winter back at home. Petra often didn't want to eat the green salad mom served nightly in the little wooden bowls set on the table. Later, it dawned on me that she didn't ever look huge or pregnant like most. We didn't talk about it, but I think she didn't gain excess weight which would be normal for her body anyway. By eating carefully, she avoided unnecessary weight gain. Not sure that salad is a favorite of hers still!

That summer went by quickly for me. In August I went to church camp at Lake of the Woods. I was a tad sad to leave mom and Petra, probably since we had been together 24/7 for two and a half months and I knew after camp we would return home. The birth of the baby was important but not consuming. I am baffled by that.

Getting mail at camp was the highlight and we all waited with bated breath to see if our name would be called. When our name was called, we got to walk up in front of everyone at lunch to get our letter. I got one letter that week, and it was from mom telling me that Petra had had her baby, that the baby was healthy but Petra had had a very hard time with the delivery. The letter probably said more but that was all I knew or would remember. We usually shared our letters, but I knew I couldn't. I was so sad Petra was "sick" but also so happy the baby had been born healthy. There was a big relief in that knowledge, tinged with sadness.

I knew the baby was going to live with a handpicked family who were friends with Petra's doctor. I knew that they loved Jesus. I don't remember giving much more thought about how this would affect Petra or our family. My selfishness makes me sad, but I also am grateful to my family for shielding me from so much hurt. Their love and protection were a huge gift and sacrifice.

Once in a while, mom would get an update on the baby and I think maybe a photo. I loved hearing the letter read aloud at the table and wished so much we could know more or even meet the little girl. At night, we would pray for her at bedtime. All we knew was that she lived in the Bay area, so we prayed she would be safe and love Jesus.

I still don't think I have ever told Pammy. I am going to have to remedy that soon.

CHAPTER 6

My Response

I cannot begin to tell you how my heart broke after I read my sisters memory. The ripples across the water are not seen until after the stone hits. I don't recall thinking of Anne's feelings, ever, during my pregnancy, it was all about myself and the boy I had been dating. Maturity took a long time to settle in. In fact it took many years to consider the ripples I had caused. I did wonder about my little girl, often looking at babies when shopping thinking they might be her. But my little sister, who was never condemning, was not my top priority. She never talked about or treated me any differently, which is beyond my ability to imagine. I don't know that I could have been the same in carrying such kindness but she carried it well.

I also remember enjoying the pool at our apartment. I remember eating lots of salad, which is not my favorite food today. It took years for me to even look at one after my pregnancy and wasn't until about 25 years later that I could eat one. I stayed quite thin during the time I carried my baby. In fact, I completed my junior year of high school and don't know how many kids actually knew I was pregnant. I still showered after PE class and only had a small bump. This is one time I could be grateful I was tall and so thin. Adding 20 lbs. only made me look more normal. In all, if I recall, I only gained about 30 lbs. altogether. Thirty pounds on someone who is 5' 8 3/4" tall is not very much, especially when you start at 98 pounds! I know, because now I weigh more than that, and can say I am far from considered fat!

Anne's heart toward me has never changed. She has remained a most amazing sister, faithful in her friendship to me and oh so fun to be around. I have learned much from her and try to be more like her. There is an exception or two. As we moved into adulthood, I found I had to still be careful because of her pranks. Her latest one has been every Thursday morning she calls me knowing I am in a Bible Study and my phone will ring, disturbing the class. It took me a while to figure all I had to do is turn off my phone, or leave it in another room. But for many times, until I realized it would be a reoccurring practice of hers, I was caught having to jump up, grab my phone and apologize at the same time. Sisters! I would never want to be without mine, except on Thursday morning from 9:30 am through 11:30 am!!

My parents stood beside me all through my pregnancy; I never heard any lectures from them. I think they knew I had learned a valuable lesson the hard way. They loved me through every tough moment I would encounter, and there were many. And of course, they too, would be facing some very difficult times. They were drawn into the ripples I had created without having a choice. My brother stood beside me, never once did I feel I had shamed him, although I knew I had. I can look back and am amazed at the love extended me by my family. The more time went by, the greater I recognized the gift I had been given.

I found out later that my father had tried to set up a bank account to help support my child and to pay for her education. It was rejected by her adoptive parents, which I understand.

This was not an open adoption. They would take my baby and I would be out of her life. However, the beautiful thing is, that was not to be in God's plans. It would be years, but I would get to meet her. I love how God works. Over and over again I would witness throughout my life, a God who is far more compassionate and forgiving then one can imagine.

CHAPTER 7

A Baby is Born

My baby was born in the early hours of the morning, August 12th. I waited a little too long before I told mom I thought I was having contractions. Well, I had been having them and they were very close together. By the time we reached the hospital, I was quickly put in a room and prepped. Normally my standing heart rate is 48 beats per minute and my blood pressure is very low as well. I'm sure, due to stress and anxiety my heart rate and blood pressure sky rocketed. Once my baby was born, the doctor could not stop the bleeding or get my pulse and blood pressure within reason. Although I did not know what was going on, it was a very tense time for all in the room with me. I was just short of crashing. But once again, God's plans for me were not yet complete, and after quite a bit of time, I began to return to normal. I had been asked before the birth if I wanted to see my baby after she was born. I said no, if I held her or even got a glance at her, I knew I would not let her go. It had been such a difficult decision for me to make but I wrote out a list of pro's and con's. My only pro was I could love her to a degree no other person could; I was her mother. Then there came the list of con's. I could love her, but how could I support her. I could love her but I would not be able to give her a father. I could love her but I could have to quit school to take care of her, and what kind of job does a drop out get? I could love her, but how could I protect her if I wasn't around? I could love her....the list kept growing. So I realized one more for my pro list. I could love her enough to give her all the advantages in life that I have had by allowing her to be placed into a loving family with two parents, a father and a mother. And that's what it all came down to. *It was not about me, this decision was about my baby.* My parents, from the very beginning, openly stood by whatever decision I would make. I knew they would help me raise my child and I also knew that, even though they would do so joyfully, they would have to sacrifice a great amount of their time, money and plans. But, I had had this remarkable child-hood. I wanted my baby to be looked at as having a mother, a father, and perhaps other siblings. I did not want her to be the 'unwedded' mother's child. No label, just loved.

So, when the nurse at the hospital came into my room and asked if I wanted to hold my baby, I told her no. As the door to my room closed, I sobbed. The consequence of my sin was to lose my firstborn. I have never cried like that again. At that moment I truly thought my heart would literally burst. I was reaping the consequences of my choices.

CHAPTER 8

Continuing Life

My return to high school for my senior year was fairly uneventful. There are always going to be those who need to meddle in someone else's life, and I definitely had those. I was surprised at the number of boys who asked me out but it didn't take me long to learn they had a specific purpose in mind, thinking I would be 'easy' due to all the rumors flying around. My first encounter was a young man a year older than I that asked if I minded if we stopped by his house on our way to our date. Of course I didn't mind but what he neglected to tell me was, his parents were gone. He invited me in and I went. It wasn't long before he had me on the couch, but not with my permission. I bit his bottom lip making him promise that if I let go, he would take me home immediately. He agreed and I let go. I was shocked, but would find out later that my first boyfriend had shared all kinds of stories, most of them not true. I think that's called 'locker talk'. So why wouldn't other boys try to take advantage? One of my other dates wanted to stop at a saw mill for a little excitement. I ended up going home early from that date as well. This was new territory that I had to learn to maneuver in.

I continued dating my first boyfriend off and on. There would be no more physical activity between us. I can't say whether it was because I knew I could get pregnant again or because I knew it was wrong. It should have been because it was not pleasing to my Savior and I didn't want to hurt Him with my selfishness again. It was probably a little of both.

In 1968 I entered Judson Baptist College in Portland, Oregon which opened a whole new world for me. For the most part, the young men were respectful, but the best part was, I got to "remake" myself into someone without a history since no one there knew me. It was a new beginning for me. I loved college, the professors, the students and the activities. I made great friends that would remain life-long friends. I dated some great guys who got to know 'me'. I felt whole. When one feels fractured, it's hard to move in the direction needed to change when everything around you is continuing on the same rail. But placing yourself in a new setting with new people who give you a new chance to be who you really want to be is so refreshing and fills you with hope. A funny thing happened when I left home. I missed my little sister. The freshness of someone so young really. She was so "her", so little sister-ish, and I missed her. To expose my new friends to my most wonderful family, I would often head home with 3 to 4 carloads of kids from college. It was a 5 1/2 hour drive, but always worth it. My parents were there with open arms and, until my mothers death 50+ years later, some of the kids would still show up to visit. What a grand statement to make about my family. My father would have loved having them come by, but he went to his heavenly home at the young age of 55. I miss him.

Dad, mom, Rick, Petra, Anne 1968

We had the little house and also what I called the 'new' house. All the boys would stay in the little house and all the girls would stay in the 'new' house. My parents were the best entertainers ever. Often times we would head up to Trudy's lake to swim, ski, explore, and then come home to a BBQ. Other times we would get a baseball game going and play all afternoon. And then of course, in the evening we would play hide and seek. If the weather was bad we had indoor games, but there was never a time to be bored. Both my parents were like magnets to my friends and made a lasting impression.

At college we had a pervert whom we called Herbert. He visited the college at times, and all of us girls had been advised not to be anywhere alone in the evenings. I had a friend named Rene, who I have to admit was a bit like myself in enjoying pranks now and then. One evening we went down to the gym and hid on stage behind where the curtains were drawn. This was not an ordinary gym, this was an old gym with many nooks and crannies, and it could be dark, pitch black dark, when the lights were off. We waited for a group of other girls whom we knew were coming down to practice on the trampoline. After the girls had arrived and as they were practicing, Rene and I allowed a chair to fall. It got incredibly quiet until someone could reasonably explain the sound and continue on their practice. After a few minutes more, we would drop some other object. This continued until the girls started screaming and ran out of the gym. Now I'm not sure why we thought it was so funny, but we did. We were just getting ready to leave the gym when we looked out the window and saw those same girls coming back with a lot of young men from the men's dorm. Our hearts were racing because we knew we would be in big trouble and possibly expelled if we were caught! Quickly we turned around and headed back to the stage. We climbed the ladder to the top beam where we laid down and stopped breathing, as much as we could. Drat, why did I have a friend who was so much like me or I so much like her!

All the lights in the gym went on and the search for Herbert the pervert began. They looked everywhere, except up. It felt like hours of just laying still, hardly breathing, and looking down to how far the floor was below us should we fall. After the search was over, we laid there for a long time before slowly climbing back down the ladder, sneaking down to the basement and exiting the basement door in the backside of the gym. The adrenalin was amazing, but the knowledge of what we had done and what the outcome could have been kept us from doing this particular prank again! But it didn't stop our pranks.

There was an upper level in our gym that was off limits because it was unsafe. The door to enter it was boarded off, but only with nails!! Nails can be pulled out rather quickly, especially if something loud is going on in the main gym. Able to come up with two hammers, my cohort and I, during basketball practice, made our way to the boarded door. Two working together is always better than one and goes twice as fast. Within a short time, we pulled the door closed behind us as we headed up the stairs to the forbidden. Exciting? Absolutely!!

Once upstairs we explored all kinds of things that had been put up there, until we came to another door that had been blocked by a large steam heater. I look back and realize that I always thought I could do anything and this was no different. It was only a steam heater, a very large steam heater, but I could move it! And I did! Only problem, I didn't secure it when I let go. Rene yelled at me and I turned around just in time to have it fall on my foot, actually my big toe. I didn't immediately feel anything until we got my foot out from under the heater. Then we saw my tennis shoe slowly turn red. Rene tried to get my shoe off but saw it was better to leave it on. It wasn't long before we had a mini geyser shooting out of my shoe. I was unable to walk on it so Rene decided to give me a piggyback ride down the stairs. Rene probably weighed 15 lbs. less than I did, and was at least 5 inches shorter. So my feet pretty much dragged as I was carried on her back. It went very well until she tripped and we fell. Neither of us were badly injured but we knew we had to have help to get me to the dorm. Somehow, we were able to get the door nailed back up and decided to go up the other stairs to the score keeping room and say we tripped on those stairs. They were not forbidden. Rene got me situated on the stair in a position that looked unnatural, then went into the gym, disrupting practice, to get the coach. I had one problem, the coach was my psych teacher and I had been dating his brother-in-law, so he knew me better than most of the professors. It didn't take him long to figure out that Rene and I were lying. I'm pretty sure he had already gone over and checked out the door to the forbidden area where we originally began our adventure. Coach Bob carried me up to the dorm and promptly put my foot into ice water. It was far colder than I could stand but he would not let me remove my foot until I told him the truth. I hate being caught by someone whose opinion I value and even more by a professor! I told the truth and my reward was to be taken to the hospital where my toe was put back into place and I was given my crutches. It's my opinion that crutches, in some circumstances, should be outlawed. My dorm room was on the second floor and I found out that going up was never a problem but coming down was not my forte! I learned the hard way that when coming down, the crutches went ahead of you, not after you had taken the step into mid air, and continued downward without anything to break your fall. It only happened once, the steps were concrete, and I lived to be able to share this bit of information with anyone interested in hearing it. Crutches first, step down, crutches first, step down.

College life was a new experience and a real cleansing for my soul. I grew in my faith, grew in my confidence and became a whole person. My old boyfriend from Eagle Point did come up to visit, and I realized he still had that hold over me. I detested it, so on his second visit, I sent him home telling him to never return. I wanted to move forward and the one thing that was preventing my moving was his visits.

Sadly, a few months after I was at college, I got a phone call from him asking me to marry him. I asked, "why now?" He had gotten another girl pregnant, a former high school friend of mine, and wasn't "in love" with her. (You have got to be kidding!!) That made no sense to me and I told him so. I was able to tell him that when you play the game and you know the rules, you determine your own outcome by how you choose to play. He was a big boy; go be responsible! It was the final hurt and he would never have any control over my life again. I was completely free to move on, and I did just that.

I was once again enjoying life. I loved going home and taking other kids with me. I loved watching Anne grow up. I had an amazing big brother. My parents were the best. My life had taken a turn in the right direction.

CHAPTER 9

Moving Forward

After college I went to work at Dammasch State Mental Hospital. The best and favorite job I ever had. Every day was different, and sometimes kept me on the edge of my seat. I was also continuing my education at Portland State University so often, when I was on night shift and had the patients bedded down, I would study in the office. One evening I was startled to feel something very sharp in the back of my neck pressing uncomfortably hard. Then I froze as I heard one of the patients say, "You killed my baby, why would you kill my baby. I want my baby back, now I have to kill you". Fortunately, we had been trained for such emergencies and I softly asked her if she was certain it had been me because I was not around at that time. Continuing to speak softly, I offered to show her my face to see if she recognized me. I knew I somehow needed to get to the panic button but at that moment, there was no moving on my part if I wanted to live. I don't know how long we talked but suddenly she said, "It wasn't you, it was my roommate. I have to go kill her"! As she turned to run back to her shared room, I slammed my hand on the panic button and took off after her. I was able to tackle her in the hallway about the time I heard the outside doors being unlocked. As strong as she was, I had more adrenaline flowing from plain fear of being stabbed with the broken glass she still carried. The help arrived, we got her into isolation, and my mind went in to that "what if" mode. What if she would have stabbed me, what if she would have killed other patients, what if I hadn't been able to hit the panic button? I hate that. It took a while to stop playing the "what if" game. The girl had been having flash-backs from drug use. I saw so many while working there, I knew I never wanted to have anything to do with drugs. The outcome was usually ugly and destroyed the person from ever being totally normal. No high was worth the horrible possibilities it offered. One of my patients was on his way to the olympics in diving and he had an incredible future ahead of him. He never got there. Instead he succumbed to the temptation of drugs and ended up ruining his life. I would take him over to the pool and watch him dive; he was so gifted. But he was unable to have a normal conversation because his mind was blown. I found it to be very sad for both him and for his family and for the contribution he could have made.

I had two roommates that lived with me at this time. Both named Judy and that was fun! What was so amazing was, they seemed to know just by the tone of my voice which "Judy" I was calling for. One was a girlfriend from school days and we had promised each other that someday we would travel Europe together. That day came. We gave ourselves time to get prepared to leave for several months. I got a second job on my off days as a vacuum cleaner phone salesperson. Now there's a job I was proud of!! One evening I was making calls to set up appointments and I dialed the wrong number. Somehow I had called Montana! How that happened I have no idea but it turned out to be one of the most interesting calls I have ever made. I found myself talking to an older gentleman and I mentioned that my grandparents had lived in Montana. In our conversation, my grandpa's name came up and the man on the other end said, "And was his wife's name Clara"? You could have blown me over with a poof! This man had been my grandparents neighbors!! Now tell me that's coincidence and I'll tell you in your dreams maybe. I love God adventures, so unpredictable and always catching me off guard!

My boss at the vaccuum cleaner store, liked his alcohol. One evening, he came in drunker then a skunk, shut the door behind him, and became aggressive toward me. Like in the tv scenes, I was moving around the desk to avoid him and my temper was growing stronger by the moment. No trace of fear. I'm pretty sure there were puffs of smoke coming out of my ears because I was so angry and disgusted with him. I don't remember what I grabbed, but whatever it was brought him to a halt. I edged toward the door, told him I would return in the morning to pick up my check, it needed to be ready, and he was not to be here. That's exactly how it worked out.

Shortly after that, I walked into a small dress shop by my apartment in Tigard, Oregon to find a dress. I had on my 'Judson Baptist' sweatshirt when I went in. I loved this shop, and since I had just walked out on my last job and was trying to save to go to Europe. I asked if they were hiring. They were not but as I was heading to the door, the shop owner came out and asked if I had gone to the college I was advertising on my sweatshirt. I told him yes and he then asked me if I was a believer. I said yes. He asked me when I wanted to start work! The answer, "ASAP"!

That was another job I enjoyed. There is something fun about having a customer come in and helping her find what looks best on her in color and fit. I became a few of my customers 'favorite' because I was honest in what I saw and what I told them. I had learned much from being in my grandmother shop, observing. Soon customers were calling before they came in, to see if I was working that day. I was sad to leave but the month arrived that Judy and I were to leave for Europe.

My months in Europe could be a book in itself. It was wonderful, opened up my mind to history, which I never liked in school, and gave me a love for travel which I would keep the rest of my life. Plus, I learned what real ice cream tastes like and I ate many foods I never knew existed. Judy and I usually ordered without knowing what it was we were getting, and I'm still grateful for that! I remember liking everything we ate and often, at the end of a meal when we couldn't figure out what we had just eaten, we would ask. Sometimes, I realized I NEVER would have placed that order had I known and I would have missed out on a very wonderful and tasty meal. The one I remember best was a rice dish with fish eyes, octopus tentacles and other seafood/fish parts. Fish eyes? I don't think so, but they were mighty good!! Judy had a meal that arrived with the entire fish, a very strange fish, head and tail and the whole body in between. We knew what salmon, trout, catfish, the normal fish for our area looked like, but this was an unknown, strange fish. She ate it and lived to tell the story of the fish.

As my life moved forward, I continued to pray that God would one day let me meet my baby. I kept track of her age, what I imagined she looked like and what she would be doing at this time of her life. I can't say I was haunted with my thoughts, but I realized I would never be able to let go of the desire to know her, to know the family she was with, and to reassure her I did not give her up because I didn't love her. I gave her up because I DID love her. I often wished I could have just 10 minutes to explain so many things. I hoped that one day, if she had been told she was adopted, she would want to meet me, but I didn't want to cause separation between her and her adoptive parents. Their family would always have to come ahead of my relationship with her. I was to blame for that.

At this particular time, she would have been four. My doctor, Dr. Bradshaw, who had delivered her, kept in touch with both me and my baby's family. In fact, she was in Dr. Bradshaws daughters wedding. I received a picture of her in the wedding and she was beautiful. Blond like me, sweet face, beautiful. I felt a sense of relief to see her face with a big smile on it. She looked happy, she looked like she was in a good family. I knew I had done the right thing in giving her a 'real' family

**The first picture I was given of my little girl
sent to me by Dr. Bradshaw, the doctor who delivered her.**

CHAPTER 10

Beginning of Monica's Story

When I reached out to Monica, asking her if she would write a part in my book she had asked me to write, she was all on board. I was so grateful, and it became a huge motivation to get the book started and finished. My first pages from her came to me and I could just imagine her as the little princess her daddy called her. I looked back at how all this took place, drawing on God's goodness to me. Here is the beginning of Monica's story, written by Monica.

"Monica, you are my girl. I got to choose you and you are my little princess. Daddy loves you so much". I can still hear my dad's voice telling me that very phrase and kissing me on the forehead good night. My relationship with my dad was a good one except for when my mother got involved, I will explain more about that a little later.

I was born August 12, 1967. I have a very funny story to tell about that, also a little bit later. My biological mother lived up in Oregon and she could not keep me due to the fact that she was very young and she wanted to ensure that I had the best life possible.

My adoptive parents, Marie and Marion Martin, lived in Pinole, California. They had a biological daughter named Connie, I was born on her birthday! What a great gift she was going to get!! My parents love to share the story about how they got a call from Dr. Douglas Bradshaw to say that I was about to be born and they could come up to Oregon and pick me up as soon as August 3. They were very excited and packed quickly to take the drive north. My sister, who was seven years older than me to the day, was so excited and could not believe that mom and dad arranged for her to get a baby sister on her birthday!

My mom always said I was a very good baby and I did not cry much. I was very chubby and giggly and I liked to have my feet tickled as well as being read to. Now, at the age of 54, I do not like my feet touched, I am still chubby and I love to read!

I remember the first time I realized that I was adopted and that meant I was a little bit different. It was my fifth birthday party and we were playing a game that involved sitting on and popping balloons. (I do not like balloons to this day!). My next door neighbor, Lisa, asked me if I missed my real mommy. It didn't really register with me at the time what she meant or was talking about, so I just ignored her and continued trying to sneak the frosting from my Barbie Doll cake. That following Sunday when I was in Sunday school another friend of mine told me that Lisa told her that my mom and dad were not my real mom and dad. I told her she was stupid and unfortunately my Sunday School teacher heard me and made me sit in the corner until my mom came to pick me up. My mom was so angry with me because I was not being a good little girl and I had said something bad in church. When we got home she told my dad that he had to spank me for being naughty. I wanted so badly to explain to her what was said to me, but she didn't care. I think she was just embarrassed because I was being naughty. But, was I really?

My family went to church every Sunday and every Wednesday we had a youth group and Bible study at our home. I enjoyed church very much because my mom and dad were always in a good mood and after church we would go out for Chinese food.

I believe I was five years old when I was asked to be in Dr. Bradshaw's daughters wedding. What an honor!! (I knew exactly who the Bradshaw's were, they played a very big role in my being adopted.) Even at my young age I knew that this wedding was an extra special event. My mom and dad had rented a great big mobile home and we would take our trip to Oregon in it. It was so fun packing up things to prepare for our road trip north. I had to be sure that I had all my Barbies, all their clothes and definitely their accessories. It was so much fun traveling in the motorhome because I didn't have to be stuck in a seatbelt! I could play dolls sitting on the floor or sitting at the little kitchen table. I could even play Barbies on my bed!! My sister, Connie, was 12 at this time. I remember sitting with her at the kitchen table in the mobile home and she had her school yearbook. She pointed out all the boys that she thought were cute. Of course at this time

I wasn't into boys, but I agreed and giggled with my sister and promised not to tell my mom and dad that she thought some boys were cute.

When we got up to Oregon, we met at the Bradshaw's house. They had so much food it was incredible. They had lunch meats and cheese, crackers and spreads, olives, rolls and a bunch of fun desserts. When we were done snacking at the Bradshaws, we went to the church to have the wedding rehearsal. It was so much fun! The bridesmaids all fawned over me, each telling me how beautiful I was. They told me I was the perfect flower girl and I looked like a princess in my pink flower girl dress. I had long blonde hair all the way down my back and the ladies were combing my hair and playing with it. They were discussing how I might wear it on the wedding day. I felt so special and adored. The next day when we woke up the first thing we did was go over to the Bradshaw's house and have a huge breakfast, which included waffles! Shortly after breakfast ended, it was time to get ready for the wedding; all the ladies were getting their makeup on and their hair done. They were all so beautiful. I was so excited to put on my pretty dress and the decorated headband to match. The night before my mom had put my hair in spongy pink curlers so I would have long dangling curls for the wedding. After we were all ready, we were swooped away to go have the pictures taken. It was so much fun taking pictures because I was getting as much attention as the bride! The photographer referred to me as 'princess' and every time he wanted me to move to a different spot he would ask,

"Princess, can you please move over to the other side of the bride"? I was more than happy to do whatever I was supposed to do because being called princess and being treated like a princess was super fun!!

At 10 years old I was still into Barbie's and my dad built me a huge Barbie house. It was amazing and it was taller than me! It included furniture, dishes, and even light fixtures. I had so many clothes for my doll that I had to use a suitcase to put them in, so my dad also built me a huge toy chest and painted it bright yellow to match my furniture and bedspread. I have always loved bright colors, and that's how I see yellow and orange, happy and bright. My room was bright and it was my happy place.

I went to several different private and Christian schools. I found out later one reason I had to leave a particular school was my mom was having an affair with the principal. I was devastated! I was leaving the school where I had my very first crush; his name was Mark. He was a twin and his twin had a crush on me. One afternoon my girlfriend arranged for Mark and I to be alone so we could have our first kiss. We sat on the couch and told funny stories about kids at school and agreed to tell everyone that we had kissed so we could be the cool couple at school. He was such a nice guy, so kind and just as nervous as I was about being boyfriend and girlfriend. Actually, we were just really great friends who could laugh and be silly together and not have a worry in the world about pressure or trying to impress one another. Three years later we would be dating again, and this time I would receive a promise ring.

The color yellow has always been my favorite because my grandparents house was bright yellow. I loved their kitchen, it was decorated with daisies. I would go to my grandparents every summer for a couple of weeks and it was always so much fun and relaxing. In the mornings I would wake up to the smell of pancakes or waffles being made. My grandma would add a little vanilla to the pancake or waffle mix and it only enhanced the smell coming into my bedroom. I would jump out of bed so fast and go into the kitchen where my grandpa would be waiting to give me a great big hug and tell me how much he loved me in Swedish. He was the kindest, gentlest most loving person on this planet. His love for God and his family was immeasurable. We would always start out days with devotions and prayer and then I would put a whole bunch of butter on my waffles and gobble them down! What a great way to start my day!

After breakfast, we would go egg hunting. My grandma and grandpa lived on a farm with lots of chickens and peacocks as well as cows. My favorite thing was to head out to the chickens' nests and hunt for eggs. I got a penny for every egg I found. After the egg hunt, I would head off looking for peacock feathers. I had the best peacock feather collection you could imagine. I would stick feathers in the waistband of my pants in back so they would stick up over my head. Then I would march around making funny peacock noises.

On Sunday we would all wake up earlier in order to get to church on time. My grandparents were very involved in church and they took pride in never missing a Sunday. I loved waking into church holding both of their hands. All the love and attention was wonderful.

It was obvious that this community absolutely adored my grandparents. My grandpa was a deacon and both by grandparents sang in the choir. My grandpa had the most amazing, deep baritone voice and I could always pick his voice out when the choir was singing. My grandma would smile down from the choir loft and give me a wink once in a while. She almost always wore her favorite daisy earrings to church, and because her favorite color was also yellow, she was often wearing yellow.

I was fortunate to have grandparents who made people feel special and loved. I miss them both but I know they are in Heaven, they are together, and they are eternally happy.

The summer of 1978 was a blast! The day after school got out my best friend Dani and I left to go spend two weeks with my grandparents. When the two weeks were over, I spent the rest of the summer with Dani at her home. She had a big pool including a diving board, and her mom would let us swim all the way til midnight. We spend every day floating around the pool talking about boys. At night we would sneak downstairs when her mom would fall asleep and watch scary movies. We would scare ourselves so bad that we would be afraid to fall asleep. Finally when the sun began to rise, we would get in a couple hours sleep.

Dani's grandfather was a pastor. That summer he asked us if we would like to help with Vacation Bible School. Of course this was a huge deal because we would be the oldest kids and, because Dani's grandfather was the Pastor, we would be treated special. It turned out to be a blast! We got to help little kids glue together people made out of gum. If a child had a perfect attendance, they would have a whole person made out of gum that they were allowed to eat later. Of course, we snuck pieces of gum, but that was ok because after all, her grandfather was the Pastor! We were in charge of handing out snacks and would take turns helping kids color while the teacher read stories out of the Bible for them to learn. Every day after Bible School was over, Dani's grandfather would take us to lunch wherever we wanted to go. Usually it was Denny's because we liked their French Fries and onion rings. After lunch when he would drop us back at Dani's home, in short order we would be back in our swimsuits and in the pool.

That summer I also joined the Silver Creek Seals. I was an excellent swimmer winning many ribbons and trophies. To this day I love to swim! Both my parents called me a water baby because of my love for the water and swimming.

CHAPTER 11

Doctors Orders

A fter I had been married and had adopted two children, a son, Jay, and a daughter, Sally, and had moved to Dallas, Oregon, I had a call from the doctor who had delivered my baby. I was a little startled at what he was asking but also very excited. It was time to introduce myself to Monica, the name given by her adoptive parents. Dr. Bradshaw said to write the letter as if this would be the only contact I would ever have with her, telling her the things that are important for her to know. He also told me to include a picture of myself.

What was important for her to know? Should I send a close up of a distance picture? Would she even be glad to hear from me? Questions were bouncing around in my head as our conversation was continuing. The years I had prayed to meet her were possibly coming to fruition. I was more than excited…and apprehensive at the same time.

His next instructions were to send the letter to Monica's mother for her to pre-read. If she then thought Monica was ready for the letter, it would be given to her by her mother. I was not to count on any connection, but again he re-emphasized he thought it was time to reach out.

Dr. Bradshaw had always remained in contact with both me and my baby's adoptive parents. Monica had been in both of his daughters' weddings, and according to him, had a standout personality. I began praying and hoping a meeting would take place in the very near future. There was another thing I had to take care of, I had to share the story of Monica with my daughter, Sally. Once again I would have to face my shame and the ripples would move out. One more person that I would have to ask forgiveness from, my own daughter.

I was a little hesitant because I was with my own daughter whom I had adopted, and now had the potential of meeting the daughter I gave up for adoption. What a crazy situation I had before me but what a blessing lay ahead of me.

I shared with Sally about Monica and I honestly do not remember her reaction. Knowing Sally, she found no fault with me; that was just her nature. She was and is a nurturer and extremely forgiving.

I spent days writing different letters, mulling over what was important, trying to choose the picture that would be the most appropriate, until finally it was time to make a final draft and get it put in the mail. If I remember correctly, the letter was about 1 page handwritten, and the picture was of me sitting on a rock in the middle of a river. Then I waited.

My first husband and I had a failed marriage and after 12 years he moved to Alaska. He had been gone for about 4 years when I wrote the letter to Monica. I tell a lot more about the reasons for my divorce in my first book, so I do not want to repeat myself again. But at this time, Sally and I were home with several of my family who were visiting for Christmas. It was Christmas Eve, the night we open our gifts after going to a Christmas Eve Service at church. I was enjoying watching the nephews and nieces play with their gifts and listening to their 'ooooh's' and 'ahhhh's' when my phone rang. After picking it up, I knew immediately it was Monica. How? I believe her voice was so recognizable, even though I had never heard it before. Goose bumps rose on my arms and something like a zap went through my body. She introduced herself and told me she had received my letter. Her mom had not read it first but gave it to Monica to read. We talked for at least 30 to 40 minutes when I suggested I call her back because it was a long distance call. I did and we talked another 30 to 40 minutes. I had so many questions, so much I wanted to know, so I asked her if I could fly her to Portland and I would pick her up for a visit. After I asked there was a little hesitation on my part. The 'what if's' began again! What if she was disappointed when she met me? What if at the last minute she changed her mind about flying to Oregon? What if her parents would be angry toward me? What if Sally did not want to meet her? What if this and what if that. I wasn't normally like this but I had never been in this position before. Then the greatest 'what if' came to mind. What if my Sally felt rejected by me. Monica was my flesh and blood but Sally was my daughter in every way, except from my body.

Why I questioned I am not sure as I have no recollection of a negative response from Sally; she was more than willing to meet and make Monica feel welcome. I was amazed at her acceptance.

Before Monica came, I set up a time to have pictures of the three of us taken at a photographers. I was anticipating how things might go, trying to think of the people I wanted her to meet, and coming up with activities that would make both Sally and Monica comfortable. What I had been praying for for years was now becoming reality. How does one thank God for His goodness? I think, at this point, I hoped to make the most out of the opportunity He was giving me, and that's just what I planned to do.

Sally, Petra, Monica–1987.
This picture was taken on Monica's first visit to meet me.

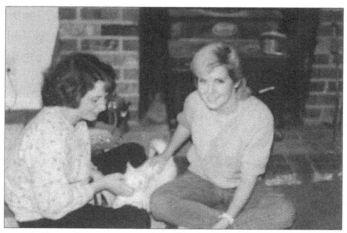

Sally and Monica on the first day of meeting in 1987.

CHAPTER 12

A Christmas Surprise
[MONICA]

*W*ow, it doesn't seem that long ago, but it was almost 40 years ago on Christmas Eve.

I was with my mom, her husband, my stepsister, my sister Connie and her husband. We were done opening presents and my mom came to me with an envelope. She said, "This will be a Christmas you will never forget", and she was absolutely right! As I was looking at the envelope and looking at the very pretty cursive writing, my mom asked me if I had any idea who the letter was from. I told her I had none. She let me think about it for a moment but then I became impatient and decided to hurry up and open the letter. First, a picture fell out and as I was reaching down to pick up the picture, I started reading the first sentence of the letter. Then I knew. I am not sure why, but I decided to go and lock myself in the bathroom to finish reading the letter. I probably didn't want everybody staring at me as I read. I finished the letter and then I stared at the picture. This beautiful, tall slender woman was my mother. The woman who had given me life. The woman who unselfishly gave me up for adoption so that I would have a better life than she could offer at that time.

You see, my family was so proud that I was their adopted daughter that it was never a secret. They told me what little they knew about my biological mother and how amazing she was to give me life. I knew she was a Christian woman and I knew she had been a young mother. I also knew she lived in Oregon and that most of my biological family lived there also.

At the end of her letter she let me know that when I felt ready, she would love to speak with me, and added her phone number. Being a fairly impatient person, I had to call, right then! I knew it was Christmas Eve and she was probably celebrating with her family like I was, but I could not wait to call!

I remember hearing Petra's voice for the first time. It was kind and I could feel the warmth through the phone. That was the best phone call I have ever made!

It was set! I was going to fly to Oregon and meet Petra! I had never flown before so I was pretty nervous to get on an airplane by myself, but I was so excited! The stewardess was so nice to me and she could see that I was clearly nervous. She asked me if I had flown before and I told her no. She then arranged for me to come sit in the front so I could be closer to her, that way she could watch over me. When she was done passing out peanuts and drinks, she came and spoke with me a while. I told her that I was going to meet my mother. She looked a little shocked until I told her my whole story. It made her cry. I will never forget that stewardess because her kindness during the flight was amazing. Her name was Brenda. When we had landed and were getting ready to depart, Brenda gave me a huge hug and told me to have a wonderful and blessed time.

As I walked into the airport, I remember looking down, I don't know why, but I think it was just me being a little bit scared. Then I heard her voice say my name. I turned my head towards the voice and I started at her shoes and slowly worked my way up until I saw her face. She was beautiful! This was my mother, and she was beautiful. I just kept repeating that in my head, I don't know why. She had the biggest smile and straight teeth. She was tall!! What on earth? There was so much I wanted to say but I didn't, I just wanted to hear her, I wanted to stare at her, I wanted to hear her laugh. There were so many questions I had and I had rehearsed them so many times, but at that moment I forgot everything I wanted to say and ask. It was like it was all just sinking in. I was with my mother. ` I hoped she didn't catch me staring at her. With so many things running through my brain, it all became a blur! I remember having thought I would not feel emotional because I had always known I was adopted. But here she was, with me!

We left the airport and headed to her home. I think I said some pretty silly things, I so badly wanted to impress her; I wanted her to like me and think I was smart and pretty, a proper lady. All the smart questions I had rehearsed to ask her and all those things I had rehearsed to tell her, to impress her, vanished.

When we had been sitting on a bench, the only question I asked her was, "When is my birthday"? Did that really just come out of my mouth? The look on Petra's face was interesting to say the least. But I realized what I had just asked and we both laughed!! My parents had told me my correct birthday all along!

CHAPTER 13

The Airport Story; Petra's Memory

The ride from Dallas to Portland Airport seemed to take longer than normal. Familiar landmarks that I knew telling me how much farther seemed to drag by, or maybe I just didn't notice them. I had planned on both Sally and I meeting Monica, but Sally choose to stay home. I let her, not knowing what she was thinking or wanting to force her into what could be a very awkward meeting. The situation was more difficult than I expected but I knew Sally knew she was very loved. There still existed a small edge in what was about to take place and I felt it in the pit of my stomach.

Arriving at the airport, I looked up the gate for Monica's flight and headed down the corridor to meet her. I told her to look for a pair of red shoes as a way to recognize me. Of course we all know there would only be one pair of red shoes on all of the feet that would be walking around the airport! But, how else would she recognize me if I didn't give her something to look for?

I was standing with the other greeters waiting for their people to come off the plane. I saw her before she entered the waiting room, and I began wondering how to introduce myself.

I was from a very warm and welcoming family but not everyone likes to be hugged, and that is how we all greeted one another. Do I shake her hand, risk the hug, or just acknowledge her by name? I chose the latter. As she got closer, I took a deep breath, exhaled and called her name. She had been looking down, I'm pretty sure looking for the red shoes I told I would wear, and then she was looking at me. Small, petite, blond, adorable, the one I had given birth to. It was all so surreal. She was a mixture of what I imagined over the years with the exception of her height. She was tiny in stature wheras I'm tall.

We stopped for a bite to eat on the way home, and as questions were bouncing back and forth, Monica asked, "When is my birthday"? I know I was stunned, trying to imagine why she would not know her birthdate, so I told her. The look on her face was so humorous, as if she were thinking "what did I just ask"! We both started laughing. The ice had been broken, we had just moved to the next level of getting acquainted. Thank you Father!!

We were almost to my home when my mind turned back to Sally. Not sure how to even introduce them, all my concerns for Sally's feelings were back. But I gave her far too little credit because, as we entered the door, Sally was there and immediately asked Monica if she would like to see her room. Off they went and for the next hour or more, I heard silence, then laughter, silence, then laughter. My heart released the fear it had been harboring and I was able to relax. They got along so well. Another gift had opened up in my life.

One morning, Monica and I went in to the bathroom mirror and began comparing our facial features. It was a hoot trying to figure out what part of her was like me and which ones we did not have in common. Our hair color, chubby cheeks, teeth, forehead eyebrows and coloring were the most similar. Maybe our eyes, I don't remember. But we laughed and once again a little of the barrier of meeting for the first time slipped down.

We looked around Dallas, went to the photographers for our picture, played games and caught up on all the years we had missed. I met her parents and sister through our conversations and she learned the reasons I had given her up. There would be many more conversations to take place over the years, but the closeness came slowly. I had just become engaged to Paul, but because he lived in Milwaukie, he did not get to meet her.

I knew I would have to prove myself to Monica regarding my intent to be in her life assuming that would be okay with her, and I knew she would have to accept me for who I was before we could move forward. I was willing to wait.

CHAPTER 14

Monica's Story Continues

*A*t 19, I was dating a man who had just recently asked me to marry him. He was a very nice man and he also had been adopted, making me think we were the perfect match. One night we went dancing and my thoughts about him being 'perfect' would be challenged. The dance club was a 21 and over, but I had already decided to sneak in. After all, the guy I was with was 25. My fake ID got me past the guards at the door but when I decided to visit the upstairs and see if I could have a glass of wine, a bodyguard stopped me. Insisting that I show him my ID, I told him I had left it downstairs or maybe it was out on the dance floor. I turned to head back down-stairs but looked back to see the body guard waving his finger at me to come back. I switched directions to go back to have a conversation with this man who I believed had believed me. I introduced myself and he in turn told me his name was Mike. Then he continued by letting me know he did not believe I was 21 so maybe we should have a discussion about that for a few minutes. A minute turned into about an hour and I had more or less forgotten about Craig. Eventually, Craig found me but before I left, Mike and I had 'somehow' exchanged *phone numbers. Over the next several months we would be on the phone often until finally he asked me out for our first date. The problem was, I needed to break up with Craig. It was the end of February and Mike and I were about to go on our date but first I spent the afternoon with Craig and told him that I didn't think we were going to work out. When Craig took me home, Mike had arrived an half an hour early, and was sitting in front waiting for me. AND, he was driving a beautiful bright red Mustang. I then took off Craig's ring and I actually told him I thought I was going to marry that man parked just in front of us! Craig was pretty angry but later in life he met and married a wonderful woman and our families are good friends today.*

A young Monica and Mike

CHAPTER 15

Continuing On In Life
[PETRA]

One of the most difficult things I had to do was to be honest with different guys that I had dated. It was always a very cautious move, and never before I got to know them well enough to trust their character. But, admitting my fault was never easy.

Five years after my divorce I met a man, Paul, who would become my husband within five months of meeting him. He was full of adventure, stronger willed than I and, in time, he proved to be my stability. We had become engaged shortly before I met Monica, and in fact, we actually met over the phone while he was visiting his sister, Susan, in Minnesota. Short as it was, it was a phone call that would become a life changer for me. We met in person in November, had two dates before Christmas, one being with his mother, his two children, my mother and Sally. A pizza parlor and a movie. I loved his mom and his children were fun to be with. Our second date was dinner. I was not ready for him to come to my home, so Sally and I met him in Salem. At dinner, after a time of small talk, Paul said he didn't know how old I was and would I please tell him. Before I could answer, Sally blurted out, "She's forty". Rather shocked, I said to

Paul, "I am not forty, I am thirty six". Sally didn't miss a beat as she continued, "She's forty. She tells all her boyfriends that she's younger than she really is", and with that slapped her hand on her forehead as if exasperated. Paul's face showed that he was in a confused state, not knowing what to believe. Once again I reassured him how old I was and once again Sally stepped in with a rebuttal. It came to an end when Paul asked me to show him my drivers license. I'm not sure if I felt insulted or relieved! At least now he would know the truth.

As I pulled out my license and handed it to him, he broke into a wide grin, looked at Sally and said, as he pointed to her, "I like you"! Their relationship would become close and too many times Sally would step into an argument we were having only to take Paul's side! Paul's love for my daughter was one of the most attractive things about him in the beginning, along with his very good looks, incredible legs, strong personality, wonderful sister and his faith.

Over the next many years I remained in contact with Monica. After she married Mike, the two of them came for a day to one of my family reunions. These were not small occasions. They lasted from Thursday afternoon golf games through Sunday, usually at a camp called Mountain Lakes Bible Camp in Oregon. The average number attending was 120, give or take a few. I loved our gatherings! We had climbing walls, zip lines, swimming, hiking, baseball, water balloon volleyball, crafts, and much more. We always ate well and in the evening we had talent (or not-so-talented) talent shows, which were often followed by sitting around a bonfire and listening to stories of our parents and their growing up years. Based on their stories, how any of those 8 kids lived to adulthood was hard to imagine. But live they did and continued to keep their families close so our desire to be together would only grow.

When Monica and Mike came to the camp, it was the first time many in my family even knew I had a daughter other than Sally. I'm sure it must have been just a little overwhelming for Monica, having only met a few of my family. Now she was surrounded by over a 100. I tried to put myself in her shoes, but I couldn't. A huge family is all I have ever known, and meeting people has always been easy for me. She and Mike did great, but have not come back to one again. I will keep asking!

I had other opportunities to visit with Monica, sometimes on a trip mom and I would take, or sometimes I would ride on a train to Benicia where Monica lived. Several times Trudy and I drove down, spent a few days with Monica and her family, and then drove farther south to where Trudy's daughter lived.

I got to see Monica's boys while they were young and as they grew into men. Monica's mom and I met at Monica's oldest son, Stephen's, high school graduation. We talked easily and had many pictures taken with Monica standing between us. It was one more hurdle I crossed knowing there were no ill feelings between the two of us. It was a warm visit.

At graduation, I felt so very proud to watch Stephen cross the stage outside to get his diploma. He would go on to become a part of the police force. We had occasionally been down there during his high school years to watch him play baseball. He pitched and was truly amazing. A few years later we watched his brother, Joseph, play as well. He played shortstop and was as good. I had the privilege of watching him play a few times while he was in college. Both boys are so talented and I am pleased to say I am pretty sure that came from my side of the family as both my parents were very athletic.

On one visit, I asked Joseph if he would play catch with me. I have no idea what he was thinking, or if he was dreading playing, but we put on our mitts and stepped outside. I think he was surprised at my ability to throw but the fun for me was connecting through something he loved and we shared. It has been so wonderful to connect with my grandsons, to get to know them. I feel privileged and honored to be accepted by them.

Trudy took the trip with me more than once and we stayed in the local motel. We explored Benicia and found it to be such a charming town. The main street, which ended at the bay, was lined with inviting stores and fantastic restaurants. Each day we would try a different one and never were disappointed. We discovered that this must be the dog capital of the world. It seemed that almost everyone out walking had a dog and every size of dog was on display! I had never seen anything like it, nor have I since. It would be an easy place to live if it weren't in California!

We took a hike at one of the parks just outside of town and as we were walking, we noticed a coyote walking parallel on the trail above us. He disappeared into some bushes, but not before we got a picture of him. The trees were just in bloom and the flowers were so fragrant that we could smell them as we walked by. Every color, size and shape of flower seemed to be represented so we took our time enjoying the day.

The hotel where we stayed had a grand piano in the front entrance, so on occasion I would sit and just play as people came and went. Trudy would call out songs if I ran out of them in my head and then I would play until she ran out of songs as well. Rarely were we there when the weather was warm enough to enjoy the pool, but we would go sit by it and pretend it was 10 degrees warmer.

CHAPTER 16

Eventful Happenings ;
A Little More History In Dallas
[PETRA]

When I moved to Dallas around 1977, I quickly made a friend. My first husband and I with our 2 children were in the park playing football when I spotted another woman playing baseball with her husband and two children. We introduced ourselves and I had found another kindred spirit. Her name was Teri and she loved adventure as much as I did. She laughed easily, was very beautiful, and her family matched mine in our ways of raising our children. Over the next many years we would have many over- the- top fun times. Tom Sawyer had nothing on us.

One day Teri and I were pretending to be spy's, (solely using our imaginations), and our task was to see if we could make it from my home to downtown Dallas without anyone seeing us. This was a crucial task if you are a spy! That meant we would have a river to cross without using the bridge, open spaces to whip through without being visible to other's eyes, and streets to cross in the speed of lightening without any cars spotting us. I hadn't had so much fun since childhood with Trudy. Let me tell you how we did it!

We were in our mid to late twenties when we started out on our adventure. The day was perfect, sun was shining, the air smelled good and the day was beckoning our need to be entertained. The kids were in school and time was ours. Leaving the house, we crossed the street to the side of our small town airport, staying behind the tall trees along the edge, hiding from any possible intruders. Coming to a main street, we had to remain hidden behind the local restaurant on the corner. It had the best peanut butter pie I have ever had and it was a favorite stop when we weren't on a mission. From there our main concern was crossing the street, timing it to coincide with a break in the traffic. We probably should have been on the Olympic team because of our ability and agility. At that time, in our town in the middle of the day, it really was not that difficult, but the mind has a funny way of taking something simple and making it complex and fun. There were no traffic lights in Dallas, only stop signs. We did not have to wait long before we were able to streak across the street to come up along side the back of our local Les Schwab Store. We then headed toward the Artic Circle where we saw some people heading our direction a little ways down the sidewalk. Naturally, the obvious thing to do was to climb the tree we were currently under. So we did, which allowed us to listen to the conversation as the people walked by. Once those possible villains had passed, we climbed down from the tree ready to face our next obstacle,….the river, or what someone with no imagination might call a smallish creek! Not that it was empty or void of water, it just wasn't a rushing current this time of year.

Crouching low and walking along the back side of the Artic Circle, we scouted out the 'river'.. This was nothing less than a James Bond moment! We would have to cross at a location not visible from the bridge, coming up from the water on the backside of a small hotel and cross directly under the bridge to avoid being seen. I love the feeling of adrenalin and I could sense Teri was feeling it as well.

It wasn't the cold water, it wasn't the swiftness of the flow, it wasn't the depth of the water, it was the slick rocks that made us stagger like drunken sailors. We slipped, fell, got wet, got up and did it all again, over and over! In time, we reached the other side. At this point we were almost to our destination, downtown! After an hour of death-defying adventure, we completed our 'assignment', and headed back to my house where we would begin dreaming up our next adventure.

1984–One of the surprises for my birthday was being picked up in a limo for a fun evening of dinner, the Konditorei for dessert, bowling and swimming. Teri had packed a suitcase with everything I would need.

We had a signal for our nights when we could not sleep. Whichever of us was feeling a little sleep deprived would call the other, letting the phone ring only once. If the other was awake, she would call back, letting the phone also ring only one time. Then, weather permitting, we would jump on our bikes and meet in town. Teri lived on the southeast side of town, I lived on the northwest side. I have no idea how many times we did this, but often it would be after midnight when we began our ride. We would ride the side streets, looking for those who were still up with lights on, conjuring up stories of what might be going on inside the home, then we would ride around the downtown just conversing about whatever. Eventually we would determine it was probably time to return to our homes, and hope for a time the next day to grab a couple of winks while the kids were at school and the husbands were at their jobs.

1981-Teri had never flown on a large jet,
so for her birthday I surprised her with a trip to Seattle.
We met the pilots for a quick picture.

1981–Teri and I in Covelo, CA where we helped my brother
track a grizzley bear. We never found the grizzley,
only what he had killed. We did find a rattlesnake and ended its life.

There were many more courageous adventures over the
years including surprise plane trips, train trips, an evening in
a limo which included dinner, bowling and swimming, hiking,

playing ball, drives to the beach and, singing *"In the Mood "* at a grade school program.

Sadly, even the best of times have an ending, and ours came when both of us were having difficult times in our marriage. Teri eventually moved and I had to start all over finding a friend who could fill the hole she left behind. That wasn't to be until Sue moved into town many years later. She was fun and very creative. We loved to walk together, she taught me how to blow snot out of my nose and to spit over a bridge. I had never been good at either until I was taught by Sue.

Sue and I ran a program at church together called G2G, standing for Generation to Generation, where we tried to connect women of different age groups. It was very successful and we did a lot of different activities. We had a cooking class, gardening class, a class on being a 'genuine' person, classes on games, whatever we could think of, we'd organize into a class. One of our favorites was wreath- making at Christmas time. It was regularly the most well-attended class and we were surprised at the incredible wreaths some ladies made.

Sue and I had a party every Christmas for our 'older' friends where we made brunch for them, read them some fun stories, and had a game which involved everyone. One year I had everyone give me a picture of themselves between the years of 16 to 24. I blew the pictures up then cut out all the eyes, noses, mouths, hair and jaw line. I put them together in groups of what I had cut out, all the noses in one group, eyes in another group, etc. The goal was for each team to put together one of the other people in the room that you knew by collecting the right parts and assembling them onto a larger piece of paper. What a hoot! And even funnier was that the person they claimed them to be looked nothing like them! I actually did this again at a woman's retreat and one group, to our surprise, put together one person's face perfectly!!

One of my favorite times with Sue and Blaine and our friends Jodie and Bob, was a canoe camping trip down the John Day River. Six days of fishing, hiking, eating, canoeing and prank pulling. One evening after we had gone to bed in our tents, my husband began passing gas. It wasn't exactly silent and he immediately blamed it on me by saying,"That wasn't me"! Please! I'm a woman of great restraint, and even if I had the need of some relief, I would never allow it to be audible! This 'gas passing' was not a one time occurrence that night. Different sounds would hit the air like a brick, shattering any chance of sleep I may have had, and each time I would hear his accusing remarks, "You know you felt that one"!! After I don't know how many times, I became rather disgusted and was ready to move him out with the coyotes, cougars and rattle snakes!! But then I rolled over and rolled right onto what I would recognize as a Fart Machine. I recognized it because we also had one but had left it at home! We now knew Sue and Blaine were trying to put a little friction in our marriage but we were not about to bite. Get even maybe, but not bite. Time would allow us that privilege, and time we had.

To look at Sue, you could never tell she was the one to teach me how to spit and blow out one side of my nose. She really does have many other talents, but those were important for me to learn.

Both Blaine and Sue are fun and slightly dangerous friends to have. Paul and I always have to be on guard when we are with them, there is never a dull moment.

Months later Sue and Blaine were out of town and being the good friends we were, we knew where their house key was hidden. Getting several bowling balls that were to be tossed out because they were cracked or chipped, Paul and I took them over to Sue and Blaine's home. We put some up in the trees, some in their water feature, some in the garden, and then went into their home. We borrowed clothes from the bedroom closet and began our project. Turning down the bed, we used the bowling ball as a head, adding to it a shirt, pants, socks and shoes. I believe we had a hat also. The perfect intruder taking a snooze had just been created. I don't remember if it was this visit or another, but somewhere in our pranks, we also switched all the kitchen drawers around. The most fun part of all we did was knowing they would get even, again, and we could hardly wait to discover what that would entail!

It wasn't too long before those bowling balls came back to us. As the weather turned colder and leaves started to fall, we began noticing the occasional patch of color in various trees on our property. Upon closer inspection, we started finding bowling balls painted to look like Christmas ornaments, with rebar hooks glued into a hole. These lovely ornaments were hanging in trees throughout our property, some hanging high and some low. Just can't imagine where they came from! Today we have what we call the 'bowling ball' tree where all of those balls hang together.

Another time we came home after our vacation very tired and we had brought our granddaughter back to spend part of the summer. I was the first one to enter the house. As I was walking through the dark kitchen into the family room, I glanced out the window because something had caught my attention. Being dark, it didn't take much to see a red light shining from up in the tree a few yards off our deck. I did a double take and it appeared to be one of the beams that come off a rifle for hunters to know they are hitting their spot on their prey. I hit the floor, crawled over to get behind the island, then ran out to where Paul and Olea were. I told him what I had seen, and he instructed Olea and I to wait in the garage and to stay out of the house. Grabbing his rifle, he circled around the woods and came up from the back side. He was carefully watching the light, as it would go off and on, until he was in position to shine his own light on the culprit! All the excitement came to a screeching halt when Paul discovered a solar butterfly, stuck up in the tree. Well now, only one couple we knew could even remotely be responsible for doing such an underhanded trick. It was payback time! Yahoo!!

Parties at Sue and Blaine's home were parties no-one wanted to miss. One time we had to come as a character from a history book and be dressed appropriately. Some of the games we played were created by the two of them, and always a hit. Sue was also the piano player for our choir and Blaine had a voice that should have been recorded and shared with the world. They greatly enhanced Paul and my lives and Sue became a real and trusted friend. It was years of surprises and fun retaliations that would take place. And then they moved. So now I wait for a Trudy, Teri or Sue to show up in Dallas to spur on my bold and courageous side, and to exercise my oddities in the most fun of ways.

A few years after Sue and Blaine moved to Montana, I got a call from Blaine asking me if I would fly out and surprise Sue. The plan was laid and I knew with Blaine involved it was going to be successful. I was to take a taxi to a specific store where Blaine had already spoken with the manager. I would be given the store's uniform so that I fit in with the store employees. Blaine was planning to take Sue to dinner, but would have to stop by to pick up an "arriving package" beforehand. It all sounded like so much fun!

When I arrived at the store, the employee's were as excited as I was. They gave me a walkie talkie and a uniform and I wondered around the store just to feel like I belonged. I kept my eye on the entrance however, waiting for Sue and Blaine to arrive while also admiring many of the items around me. Then it happened. "Please bring the parcel for

Billmans to register 2". That was my clue. I was the deliverer! The empty box was huge so I could easily stay hidden behind it, but there was a glitch. Sue was talking on the phone! I kept peeking around the box and Blaine and I were communicating with our eyes, but Sue kept talking! Finally Blaine removed the phone from her hand and asked her to please grab the package from the clerk while he paid for it. As she took the box from me, I turned to walk away but glanced over my shoulder to see if she had even noticed me. Then the screams began as she determined who I was. We hugged and had most of the employees watching and laughing. It was wonderful. Had to travel a long way to get a prank in, but it was ever so worth it!!

Sue, Blaine and Paul on one of our trips to Montana.

I have had and have many wonderful friends, both past and present. Not all are of the the adventurous nature, the ones who take a challenge as something to be met and who are not afraid to just have fun in life, regardless of our age. Some actually keep me sane and normal. It's good to have a mixture!

I have close friends in our Bible Study, close walking partners, a close friend whom I pray with on Monday nights, wonderful neighbors who provide us with 'grandkids', a terrific 'game night' group who get together once a month for dinner and games, my tennis friends, my younger friend who comes up to spend time 'hanging out' and doing a Bible Study together, and I am also privileged to be a godparent. There are many blessings in my life that I never want to fall short of recognizing. I also have a husband who gives and gives. He allows me my independence yet fills our time together reminding me of how much I am loved.

CHAPTER 17

An Update Of Monica

I have a younger sister, Dawni. We have the same father but different mothers. Dawni is two years younger than me and just the sweetest lady I have ever known. She has two daughters that are the same age as my boys, Stefano and Joseph.

When we first became aware of having a half sister, we made the decision to drive to Reno, Nevada and meet at a casino. I will never forget the waitress in the casino walking by me, taking a double look and being quite bewildered. Then, after walking past, she walked backwards and looked at me again, saying, "You have a twin right around the corner". Both my husband, Mike, and Dawni's husband, Jeff, looked around the corner at each other and at Dawni and myself and were shocked! We really did look almost identical!! When Dawni and I saw each other for the first time we were so excited and so giggly and silly, we just could not believe that we were meeting and we looked like twins!

We have a great relationship and each time we talk on the phone it's as if no time has passed at all between conversations.

Dawni and her husband live in Oregon, the same state where Petra lives. Dawni runs a cute little gas station/convenience store and it keeps her very busy. Her husband is much like my husband, both working in the construction business. My hope is when Mike retires we can take mini road trips to Oregon because that is where all my family lives.

It has been such a fun and exciting time getting to know family members because they are amazing! I have so much love surrounding me, I am one very lucky lady.

Monica and Dawni.
It was shocking to see how much they looked alike.

CHAPTER 18

Monica's Family [Monica]

O ne really nice thing has been the ability to call Petra with things that I'm going through with my two sons. I have two amazing young men, Stefano, who is 26, graduated from college and is now a sheriff. He is also engaged to a beautiful young lady by the name of Rachel, and their wedding will be in July of 2023. (Actually, they are married, but that's not for public knowledge at this time. Shhh.)

Joseph, who is 22 and in his senior year of college, would like to be a EMT Firefighter. Petra's husband, Paul, is a retired firefighter having worked in Portland, OR and she shared the most amazing pictures with me of Paul on a fire. They were actually a little bit scary but amazing. Joey, as we call him, was so excited to see the pictures, he had me print them out for him so he could carry them with him to stay motivated. It's hard getting into fire fighting! I do remember right before Stefano entered the police academy, I was scared out of my mind. I was so hopeful that he wouldn't go that route but he did, getting his degree in criminal justice. Sometimes one just has to let go and trust the others judgement.

I have been married for 33 years to a wonderful man named Mike. We have definitely had our ups and downs, but the general trend it up. He is my best friend and my soulmate. To be honest, I don't feel like that every day, but most of the time I can say this in truth!

Mike is the main breadwinner in our house and he works so incredibly hard. Hopefully he will get to retire within the next year. We just need to get Joe through this last year of college and then we can both relax a little. As for me, I enjoy walking dogs and I also work with autistic children part time at a K-8 school. That is another thing Petra and I have in common! She taught in Special Education and she loves animals. She often sends me the best pictures of deer in her front yard eating what she feeds them. That makes my heart so happy!

I love being active because I feel like if I slow down, the world is going to stop and I will have not done every-thing I want to do. I believe Petra is the exact same way. I've learned that we both are a little bit stubborn and headstrong. I love the honesty that the two of us share. I cannot wait to be a grandma because I hope I am as energetic and funny as she is. The beautiful part about Petra and my relationship is there is absolutely no judgment. I have shared things with her that most people would judge and she absolutely does not. She gives me advice, words of wisdom and offers prayer. She is actually a true meaning of a mother. All the love and caring and no judgment. She has let me move at my own pace with our relationship and I don't even know if she knows how much she has taught me. I am still learning how to walk with the LORD and she has been so encouraging and kind and thoughtful with my experience. Even though we don't get to see each other a lot, I know I am in her heart as she is in mine. I never ever question her love and devotion to me because I feel it. I feel it in my heart, in her voice, in her words and her laugh. Petra is the woman I strive to be and to me that is what a mother is. A mother should be someone you want to mirror. Your mother is someone that you should want everyone to compare you to. I am so blessed.

CHAPTER 19

We Are Alike! [Monica]

It is so funny as time has gone so fast. The bond that I have created with Petra so many years ago feels like only a couple of months ago. Over the years I have found that I want to call her and share my life with her and share my kids' lives with her. The ups and downs.

I love getting her advice and hearing her laugh, she has the best laugh! I love sharing stories with her because it just shows how our personalities are so much the same. The things we feel strongly about, the things we find comical and the things that we are passionate about. We really are the same person!

Not too long ago I was sharing a story with her about my friend, Justine. Justine and I have a horse named Mr. Positive. We were moving him to a new stable and getting him settled in when Justine decided she was going to crawl up on the fence and take a picture of Posie in his new environment. I told her, "You know I think that the wire going across the fence is electric." She didn't think so and said she would be just fine. So instead of listening to me, she crawled up on the fence to take the picture of Posie. Whiile sitting on the corner of the fence, of course she got a good charge of electricity sent through her body. When I realized she was just fine, I doubled over with laughter. She had a nice little red mark on her right cheek on her bottom. Now most people would be alarmed that their friend got electrocuted, but not me, I just laughed and laughed, and kept on laughing until my stomach hurt.

When I shared my story with Petra, she was laughing pretty hard as well and I knew we had the same sense of humor. We might be a little bit off but we realize when something's funny that humor can't stay inside. You have to laugh!

It has been fun sharing stories of the silly things I did in high school and hearing her just laugh and then compare notes. One of those stories went like this.

In high school we would go out at night and go 'cow tipping'. (That's when you try to knock over a cow that is sleeping.) Not always did it go so well, there were many times I found myself slipping and sliding in cow poo, fresh cow poo! Worse yet there was a time I got chased by a very mad cow! But, oh man, it was so much fun! Only once did we have a farmer come out with his rifle and he was super angry. I ran, probably faster than I had had ever run. Ever!

Another fun thing we did in high school was called 'ice blocking'. At that time, we were able to buy big blocks of ice and we would put a towel over it, that way we could sit on the ice and go down a hill that had a little river at the bottom of it. The point of the game was to fly down the hill and get as close to the river without actually going into the river. The river was so cold, believe me, no one wanted to land in it! Worse yet, it was extremely hard to stop the block of ice we were sitting on, but the chances of not being able to stop increased the challenge of riding the ice. It was so much fun!

As I told my stories to Petra, she would just laugh, and then tell a story of her own, something similar and sometimes just a little bit naughty, but always funny.

Monica and Mike. I am so pleased she married so well!

Mike, Joseph, Petra, Monica and Stephen.
A wonderful family I became a part of.

CHAPTER 20

Winding Down [Petra]

L ife has included a great many things for me, challenges, heart break, joys, adventures, breath taking moments, stimulation, motivation, growth, and failing and accepting all that has come my way. But when I think of all God has given me, I am overwhelmed at His goodness. I come from a family who allowed me to understand what it is to be loved, I was given a second chance at marriage to a man who has filled me with a love I could not have imagined, I was given the privilege of adopting two children who were adventurous and fun, and kept me young. And I've been blessed to meet and have a relationship with the baby I gave up at birth.

I know I could write book after book about my life but none will ever be as healing for me as authoring my previous book and now this one. I have learned so much about myself, revisited emotions and gotten to relive them differently because I am now on the 'other side', and I have been reminded that the God I worship and adore is a Great God full of compassion and full of grace just waiting to be poured out on anyone willing to receive it. I am willing.

The last paragraph I received from Monica as we worked on this book was so touching. I read it over and over, thinking back to the times I dreamed about the possibility of meeting her. It is real proof that the Creator has plans we cannot begin to comprehend until they happen. This ride of faith was far better in its outcome than expected. The following paragraph is a writing of hope and encouragement for other mothers who have been separated from their baby, and are living with the "I hope" in their hearts.

CHAPTER 21

From Monica

*G*etting to know Petra through the years has been amazing. I couldn't have asked for a more kind and whole heartedly honest, sweet and loving person to be my mother. I have to be honest and say for the first couple years of getting to know each other I wasn't sure how I felt because I didn't know if what I was feeling was love or curiosity or, in my mind, am I supposed to love this person because she is my biological mother. It didn't really hit me until I became pregnant with my first son, Stefano. As my belly grew and I felt this little one kicking and squirming inside me, I started to understand the love that a mother truly feels. Then I knew I loved Petra and I loved her so much that I wanted her to be a part of my life, to share my joy in becoming a new mother. I also began to understand how hard it must have been for her to give me up for adoption, the most unselfish act a young mother can do.

I love you so much!

Monica and I at Joe's baseball game.

Epilogue. [Petra]

I am very blessed to have two daughters who have given me a full life. Although one lives nine hours east and one nine hours south, we have phones and FaceTime in between visits. God is good and He is good all the time. My life is a testimony to this fact.

Sometimes it's easy to ask 'why'?. There are going to many times in this life when we will never know the answer to the fullness we would like. But other times, like my story about Monica, the 'why' was answered in a fashion I could have never imagined. I find it so curious how God can take a sin like mine and turn it into a blessing. What I did in becoming physically involved before marriage was wrong but, perhaps because of my continued faith in Him, God gave me an opportunity to be forgiven and restored. Repentance is a powerful action, offering healing and a new beginning, a chance to start fresh. Out of repentance comes the beauty from ashes. In sharing our stories, others are touched and steered in the direction of their own restoration. I love when I speak at events and women come to me and begin opening up regarding their own stories. Some have said they are walking in my younger shoes at that moment, so we pray. Others seek a response to something that is happening in their family. And there are those who I just hold and cry with. One of the greatest blessings that comes with opening up your life with others is there is nothing for anyone to gossip about. An open book removes the lies or secrets that someone can conjure in their mind and provides them with an accurate story.

I hope you have enjoyed reading my life's adventures. I can say today that there are things I would have changed, but again, had they changed I would not have this story to tell. Blessings can happen from bad experiences, it all depends how one chooses to approach life.

If you would like to leave me any comments, you can leave them at lessonsingrace@gmail.com. Thank you.

Revelation 21: 4-5
He [God] will wipe every tear from their eyes. There will be no more death or mourning or crying or pain, for the old order of things has passed away." He who was seated on the throne said, "I am making everything new!" Then he said, "Write this down, for these words are trust-worthy and true."

Revelation 17:14
They [the evil kings] will wage war against the Lamb, *but the Lamb will triumph over them because he is Lord of lords and King of kings–and with him will be his called, chosen and faithful followers."*

I cling to these versus as my hope. I believe what God says God will do and someday I will be taken to live where there will be no tears, no pain, no mourning or death! I will be living in God's presence and in His perfection for eternity! This thrills my heart.

I want to end with a story from years ago that has been an example of the kind of person I want to be to others.

There was once a little girl who lived with her family and was loved greatly. Next door lived a man and wife who had no children, but loved children. The little girl enjoyed her visits with the woman next door because she was treated so grown-up. One day the woman next door invited the little girl to have dinner with her. The little girl was so excited and dressed in her very best to join her neighbor. The woman had set the table with her best china dishes and goblets as well as having prepared a meal fit for a queen. The two of them had wonderful conversations over the meal and eventually, it was time to clean up. The little girl dutifully carried over her dishes to the sink and then asked if she could help washing them. The woman said she would be delighted to have the help. The little girl washed the dishes with great care to be sure they were clean and placed in the rack correctly. Without warning, one of the dishes slipped from her hand and shattered on the floor, sending broken pieces everywhere. Unable to control herself, the little girl broke into tears, sobbing at the horrendous mistake she had made. The woman, moved by the little girls reaction, took her in her arms and told her, "Do you see all those broken pieces? They are just stuff, stuff that breaks and can be replaced. But you, you are more than stuff, you are irreplaceable and extremely valuable". After she held the little girl for some time, she continued on, "Dry your tears and finish your task. Then we will do something fun together." The little girl never forgot this lesson and as she grew into an adult, she tried to hold lightly the 'stuff' in life, and hold with care, hearts of those who crossed her path.

I was that little girl, and my neighbor, Rosemary, taught me a lesson that has been imbedded in me for life.

To God, we are so much more than "stuff", we are a soul and life that matters to Him. And when we stay focused on

Him, we are filled with a joy that only He can give. Our way of looking at life can make a difference in those we meet, and in who we become.

Our Attitude reflects our heart. It is our choice how we approach tough times. We need to remember....Faith doesn't get you around trouble, it gets you *through* it!!

Petra (birth mother), Monica, Marie (adoptive mother).

What a blessing to see how God has worked.

Petra and Anne. My sister has been a blessing to me from the day she was born. It just took me awhile to recognize the incredible blessing I had been given.

Petra, Rick, Anne. I could not have better siblings had I ordered them myself!

Paul and I attending Paul's brothers wedding.

Paul, Olea (granddaughter) and Sally. Sally and Paul have a wonderful bond. Many times she took Paul's side when Paul and I would be having a slightly heated discussion. I laugh now, but I didn't then!

Trudy and I. I couldn't have a better travel partner and friend!
Everywhere we go is an adventure. I am always looking forward
to the next time we head off to the places unknown to us.

Trudy and I on one of our adventures.

Petra and Paul. One of the best gifts I have been given is my husband.
He has been my encourager in wrting my book, showing kindness
and support in every way. He has been patient when I have felt sleep
deprived, refusing to push those buttons which tend to set me off.
He has held me when I cried, and laughed when I read him
some of my stories. He is a joy in my life!

Monica has been married for 33 years to the love of her life. She has
two amazing sons and she and her husband are so incredibly proud of
them. She is involved in animal rescue and feels so fortunate to get to
live the life she had always dreamed. One of the absolute best things
that happens to her is when people compliment her and tell me how
much she looks like her mom, Petra. She feels very blessed in life.

Anne married her high school sweetheart and celebrated their 45th anniversary. Her current adventures are building a remote cabin with her husband in Alaska and section hiking the Pacific Crest Trail with a friend. Her greatest joy is having a family who loves one another and Jesus. She and Petra, although opposites in many ways, share a very close and humorous relationship. They talk about anything and everything and enjoy laughing about their many "movie moments".

CPSIA information can be obtained
at www.ICGtesting.com
Printed in the USA
BVHW031826240223
659186BV00002B/44